T0031193

LAURA'S DESIRES

LAURA HENRIKSEN

LAURA'S DESIRES

NIGHTBOAT BOOKS
NEW YORK

ISBN: 978-1-643-62195-1

COVER DESIGN AND INTERIOR TYPESETTING BY KIT SCHLUTER
TYPESET IN ADOBE CASLON PRO AND SCHOOLBOOK

CATALOGING-IN-PUBLICATION DATA IS AVAILABLE
FROM THE LIBRARY OF CONGRESS

NIGHTBOAT BOOKS
NEW YORK
WWW.NIGHTBOAT.ORG

To Morgan Võ, my friend and desire

CONTENTS

I.

Dream Dream Dream

if memory is the act of bearing witness
if jesus was born at midnight
if la la la la la la la la lalalallllaaaaaaa
then the dream is a friend driving us somewhere

—AKILAH OLIVER
"green fibs"

O NE LEGEND I'VE ALWAYS FOUND COMPELLING warns that if you die in your dreams, you die in real life. This interstitial space between worlds, residing for a time in both, it's hard to believe that an event in one could occur with no consequences for the other, that I could live on after my dream self dies. But then perhaps, like a cat, I have many dream selves. If not unlimited dream selves, at least enough to spare a few.

I WAS FIRST INTRODUCED TO THIS NOCTURNAL THREAT by a very bad babysitter. I adored her, her barrettes, the streaks in her hair, the way the performance of care seemed totally alien to her. I begged her to tell me more, and she obliged, either indifferent to the fear it clearly provoked in me or motivated by it. All my false courage drained from me after she left in the evenings, and by night I was too terrified to close my eyes, afraid of both what I might see in my dreams and what I might fail to see around me in the dark of our bedroom while my sister and I slept. Now I am a fairly heavy sleeper, a trait I find embarrassing, especially when in company. A secret world continues around me of night activity and sound, each event unrepeatable, and while I am physically present for them, I am fundamentally excluded, lost in dreams, exclusive in their way too. Perhaps it is this anticommunal element of dreaming that interests me, their temporary but acute isolation. But then of course they aren't entirely anticommunal. There is, for example, the particular intimacy of dream disclosure, a classic if often transparent excuse to text someone on your mind. And then perhaps they will tell you they dreamt of you too. You dreamt the same thing at the same time.

IN SELENA'S "DREAMING OF YOU," I'VE ALWAYS UNDERstood it to be the case that it's the power of Selena's dream love for the "you" that brings them together in the seventh verse. So far as the listeners know, no event in waking life has transpired to explain the sudden change in the relationship from one occurring only at a distance to sharing a bed. Perhaps she visited her love in their sleep as well, perhaps her dreams were like a spell, calling a wish to life. Or perhaps the story is much darker, as she closes with the phrase "endlessly endlessly dreaming," which could be understood to mean that none of this has taken place in waking life, that she remains alone in her fantasy. Or it could mean that through this love all of life is now like a dream.

O R FRANK OCEAN SINGS, "I THOUGHT THAT I WAS dreaming when you said you love me," this fantasy event of a love confession—I imagine it taking place in a pool—rendering reality in that moment unbelievable, too good to be true. But then immediately he clarifies, "the start of nothing," like waking up from a dream in the same room you fell asleep in, still yourself, circumstances unchanged.

THAT OSCAR WILDE QUOTE, "THE ONLY THING worse than being talked about is not being talked about," but instead of talked about, dreamed about. I love the idea that I might haunt someone else's dreams. It would be such an efficient form of revenge, proof of my continued significance in an old friend or flame's interior landscape, even if now reduced to a symbol, without the waking life humiliation of admitting that I care if I am remembered or forgotten, if I am stripped of my signifying power. At the same time I am troubled to have no power over Laura's dream behavior. What if I am making a fool of myself? It keeps me up at night.

THE TROUBLE THAT ANIMATES "ALL I HAVE TO DO
Is Dream" by the Everly Brothers is the power of
longing, the fear that longing might grow to such
a fever that life is dreamed away, waking reality eclipsed by
a vision of love. In a way it calls its own bluff, doubts the

foundational premise that dreaming alone is sufficient, can be the one thing, the end of nighttime loneliness. I learned that when you're deep, deep asleep, a part of your brain tells the muscles in your body not to move in response to your dream, so that you might lie there still while in your mind you are being chased, taking a test, speaking with a dead relative, having sex with a former lover or casual acquaintance or someone you saw on tv. This is also the cause of sleep paralysis, waking before the connection between your brain and your muscles is reestablished. I've experienced it very infrequently, and only once did I see the shadowy figures I've heard described by more regular sufferers. I was an undergraduate home for summer break, asleep in the afternoon on a green couch in a rented cabin in Northern Arizona. My high school friends were outside, riding down hills on borrowed bikes. We were all still a little in love with each other, still measuring our desires and capacities through the way these desires and capacities reflected off each other's, but also already growing apart, in a trajectory that I'm afraid would only continue. A few years after that summer, it became clear to me and everyone who knew me that I needed to do less amphetamines, which was difficult, and one way I attempted to achieve this goal was by visualizing this lake I had sat beside one night on that trip, the moon above brushed by thin, vaporous clouds. That whole campsite later burned down, and I never could disabuse myself of the suspicion that there was some connection between the figures I saw in my moment of sleep paralysis and the fire. They had just sort of hovered between the wall and an open door connecting the living room and hallway, at the very edge of my sight, as if waiting for something.

11

I TAKE A WORKSHOP ON DREAMING WITH JACKIE WANG. In it, she says that when a person is approaching death, they are more likely to be visited by the dead in their dreams, but that these visits come as a comfort, a warm haunting, a slow ferry to the land of the dead. She's brought a small pink harp with her, and we take turns plucking its strings.

TOWNES VAN ZANDT SINGS, "PERHAPS WHEN YOU watch all your dream lovers die you'll decide that you need a real one," but I can't imagine what kind of lover he would have been, and now he's dead too.

IN DREAMS I AM NOT MYSELF. IN MY FAVORITE DREAM, I am an owl flying over the ocean, although I don't know that owls are ever so close to the coast, in my imagination they are only ever in winter forests. It's night, or rather it's dark, and I'm looking at the orange lights in the windows of the waterfront properties lining the shore. A storm is picking up, and a little black bodega bag is caught on the wind. I'm watching it fly. Then I'm perched on a streetlamp rising up from the ocean.

SOON AFTER WE STARTED DATING, THE PERSON WHO would become my husband went to visit his grandmother on what would become her deathbed. Like a kind of introduction in absentia, he described my owl dream to her and she nodded. A few weeks later I went with him to meet her. We had to cross the longest bridge I had ever been on to get to the hospital—we were driving over the surface of a bay for twenty minutes maybe, so bright in the sun it felt more like passing over a field of snow—and its expanse made me dizzy, ecstatic, which felt at first inappropriate under the circumstances, but then also like a supremely logical reaction to the physical manifestation of transition. When we arrived, I bought her potato chips at a vending machine. She was very kind to me. The more I think about it, the more I suspect the dark sky in the owl dream did not represent night at all, but a different kind of day, or a day on a different planet. Or it might have prefigured a storm. Or maybe it was the low cloud cover of a storm already rolling, endless, heavy, beautiful, a pervading scent of petrichor, a world like an unstable life, repeatedly transformed.

15

I TELL A FRIEND I'VE BEEN WRITING THIS POEM ABOUT dreams, and he plays "When I Stop Dreaming" by The Louvin Brothers for me. This song, which speaks of an earthbound and mortal lost love, over before the song began, is a departure from the devotional bluegrass gospel music the singers are more widely recognized for. Ira Louvin designed the cover for their most famous album, *Satan Is Real*, which depicts the brothers at a quarry dressed in white suits and straight black ties, an enormous plywood devil set behind them over the rocks, several small fires burning from hidden tires. The brothers face the camera, their arms stretched out, singing. The gesture is inviting, entreating almost, as if they had just opened the door to their home in hell and were asking me to step inside. I look it up, Ira was the brother with the drinking problem, he was violent and abusive, his third wife Faye shot him four times but he survived, only to be killed alongside his fourth wife, Ann, by a drunk driver in Missouri, 1965. I think there were some rumors that Ira was a Satanist, but I don't remember for sure. I read that when the brothers performed together, at times they would switch their harmonizing and each sing the other's part, such that it would be impossible for the audience to determine to whom each voice belonged. I wonder what kind of relief this temporary escape from the self may have provided, or if it only made things harder, as the note eventually faded, the song inevitably closed.

I N AN ESSAY ON BEING UGLY, ON REFUSING TO PURSUE a type of beauty that comes through constant, punishing submission to standards designed to test how much pleasure you will deny yourself in an attempt to approximate a toxic internalized fantasy of what it is to be desirable, fuckable, marriageable, Virginie Despentes writes, "I'm not into giving a hard-on to men that don't make me dream." I underline this statement as I read on the train, imagining what it would be if a person's desirability were measured by how much they set you dreaming, how wild they made your dreams.

"DRIP TOO HARD" PEAKED AT NUMBER FOUR ON Billboard's Hot 100, but for me it was the song of the year. The first time I heard it I was listening to Hot 97, or barely listening, I was in my sister's kitchen, washing dishes or cooking, I don't remember, music in the background. Later that day I felt very tired, and so decided to take a nap, a fitful kind of sleep I normally avoid. Even though I had barely registered hearing the song earlier, its hook—the loop of a guitar line so manipulated as to hardly be recognizable as a plucked string—was irresistible to the extent that it coated my dream like moisture in a cave, and I woke up with the song in my head, although I couldn't remember what it was. I received its pulse with the gravity of an ambiguous prophecy. Lil Baby closes the song's chorus with the repeated line, "Every other night, another movie getting made." In a literal sense the many movies can be understood to be amateur porn, joyful documentation of regular celebrations of desire and luxury and beauty. At the same time, I am interested in the way the movies are also dreams. Diamond-studded, insistent, hallucinogenic dreams.

MERLEAU-PONTY WRITES, "THE FEELING OF eternity is hypocritical; eternity feeds on time... Eternity is the time of dreams, and the dream refers back to the day before, from which it borrows all of its structures." To me the way dreams simultaneously combine before, now, and something else neither before nor now does not so much show eternity's limitations, as it shows eternity's constitutive parts, which include us and our days. Dreaming does feel like an eternity outside of time, but then so does waiting to fall asleep, or waiting for a lover's return, or waiting for someone to die.

I N A CAR IN CALIFORNIA I LISTEN TO MY SISTER SING along with Nancy Wilson, "These dreams go on when I close my eyes / Every second of the night I live another life." "These Dreams" might be Heart's most glittering, technically lush power ballad. Nancy was sick when she recorded the song, which changed the quality of her voice to something deeper, more gravelly. Producers afterwards asked her if she could just get sick again. Who isn't compelled by the idea of leading another life? A life without consequences, outside a clear causal chain, instead of the one where we need money to live and get sick and often feel misunderstood and thwarted in our desires.

ISTENING TO JACKIE DISCUSS DREAMING I CON-
sider the possibility that the kind of freedom
afforded in dreaming might offer an example of a
kind of freedom we could pursue for each other in waking
life. In dreams I can recognize a place or a friend, for
example, even if their appearance is transformed, such that
it is both a kind of reunion and a first meeting. This defa-
miliarizing simultaneity allows for an unstable complexity
of identity, a fundamentally uncategorizable uncertainty,
that if I offered to everyone I know, if I incorporated into
my language, would make me a much better friend, lover,
neighbor. It would be a way to do what Simone Weil asks
us to when she writes, "Every being cries out silently to be
read differently." The same is true for my self: in dreams I
can change constantly, I can be unfixed, and in this way
imagine a deeper stability, not contingent on the illusions
of my attachments, but the depth of my intricate and flex-
ible connections. In dreams it's easy to get a little cosmic in
my yearnings, particularly when I'm a little cosmic in my
yearnings all the time.

L EOS CARAX'S *MAUVAIS SANG*, ALSO KNOWN AS *THE Night Is Young*, is about, among other things, an STI spreading across France that is only transmitted when lovers have sex for reasons other than romantic love. A group of thieves are blackmailed into stealing the cure from the office of a greedy pharmaceutical company. Alex, a young card shark played by Michel Piccoli, is recruited to the case as a replacement for his father, a legendary criminal who died before the start of the film. While initially disinterested in the endeavor, and more generally in the role of heir apparent to his father's dynasty, Alex is persuaded when he meets Anna, the lover of one the blackmailed organizers, played by Juliette Binoche. Much of the rest of the movie takes place at night, semi-private hours through which Alex and Anna stay up to flirt while Anna's partner sleeps in the other room. I experience these scenes as offering a potential approach to lucid dreaming, the approach being to just stay awake and do the things at night you want to do during the day but for a range of reasons, both social and personal, you can't. In one particular long night of wakefulness, Anna lies on a couch, depressed, and asks Alex to pick a record to put on. The pressure of the moment is too much for him, so he says they should rely on the mystical intuition of the radio, which will play just the right song for them as soon as he turns it on, "like magic," he promises. It doesn't work, or it takes three tries: first there is only static, and then a sad song about regret that maybe is the right song for their situation, but not the one he wants to hear (in it Serge Reggiani sings "Her heart, my heart, and the dying hope, work gradually separates the night, the day. We are always looking for each other"), and then finally what Alex has been looking for all this time, David Bowie's "Modern Love." Upon hearing the opening bars, as if awoken to an emergency, Alex erupts from the room—Piccoli was formally trained in circus performance and clowning, which brings to his gestures an excess beyond realism that is both more dreamlike and more real-feeling—and the camera follows alongside him, the song shifting from diegetic sound to a kind of divine intervention into the night scene. At first he moves as if in pain, clutching his gut and stumbling, but soon he is just running, a plane preparing to take-off, possibly to crash. The song cuts off and Alex stops, as with a sudden realization, he turns back, the camera close on his face this time as he sprints along the deserted street. When he arrives back to the squat, Anna's seat on the couch is now vacant. Perhaps she went to bed, or maybe morning has arrived and she's gone to start her day. He stares at the indentation of her absent reclining body, the bits of trash she left behind—a blue tissue, a cigarette—and then he lies face first where she used to be, as if in touching her detritus he might touch her, as if in assuming her former place he might become her, as if time might stop and swallow him. He gently holds the tissue in his hand, like a fragment from a dream that through some miracle remains in the morning, a kind of proof beyond use.

"ANOTHER NIGHT, ANOTHER DREAM, BUT ALWAYS you," really does it for me as a romantic conceit. I like to imagine what the essential quality must be in this "you" that makes them recognizable across nights, across dreams, somehow both reliable and mysterious, inescapable and unattainable, always returning, never fettered. "I feel joy, I feel pain, cause it's still the same," studio singer Karin Kasar sings and frontwoman Patsy Petersen lip syncs. In the video, which has a typical black and white 1990s industrial ambience, the disembodied dream lover is represented narratively as a DJ who Patsy listens to every night, up on her Berlin roof with her radio, wondering who and from where the voice emanates, broadcasts. The radio as a metaphor for dreams is a good one, something that perhaps can be explained mechanically but whose mechanical explanation is nevertheless insufficient, failing to account for the mystery of someone speaking to you in your room who is not in your room, this shadow between presence and absence, communal and private, intimate and alone, real and imagined, sending messages to you and to anyone else who is open to receiving them, although each listener will interpret the signal differently, like Anna and Alex don't hear the same song when they hear "Modern Love," like you and I might not hear the same song when we hear "Drip Too Hard." "Another Night," was released in the United States the same year Selena's "Dreaming of You" was: 1995. There was something in the air.

24

MANY ARGUE THAT *A NIGHTMARE ON ELM STREET 3*: *Dream Warriors*, which features a score by Angelo Badalamenti, is the best in the franchise, and that is true. The idea of banding together in sleep through group hypnosis so that you access your dream powers, which include incredible gymnastic ability, to defeat an evil that has haunted your community for generations has, I think, an irresistible, perhaps universal, appeal.

WHILE I HAD ASSUMED THAT URBAN LEGEND "If you die in your dreams, you die in real life" connected to more ancient mythology—which maybe is still true—I later learned that it was popularized in the 1980s through a deeply upsetting news cycle. From 1981 to 1988, 117 refugees living in the United

States, largely Cambodians who fled the Khmer Rouge regime and Hmong who fled the Laotian Civil War, died of sudden unexpected nocturnal death syndrome, which later came to be understood as Brugada syndrome, a disruption of the heart's normal rhythm in sleep. A *New York Times* article from 1981, reports that doctors were exploring what they called "Oriental nightmare death syndrome." Even more racist than it sounds, the idea wasn't that surviving genocide and war might lead to nightmares so terrifying as to be literally unbearable, but rather that this was a problem of social and religious development, "their religion is animist, governed by spirits and manifestations of the soul. Terror Induced by Nightmare." Wes Craven explained that he read a story about one of the many refugees who died in their sleep; a little boy whose family had been forced to migrate from Cambodia to the United States. His parents recounted that before his death, his nightmares were so severe, he was afraid to fall asleep. This tragedy was the inspiration Craven adapted to tell a story about a group of white suburban teenagers tormented in their dreams, hunted by the monstrous manifestation of their parents' American vigilantism. I haven't watched all or even most of the series, and so don't know how it ends, but based on my understanding of horror franchises in general, I suspect that it doesn't. That instead it must necessarily remain open to remain potentially profitable, a relentless cycle of violence, propelled by rage and repressed guilt and fucked up desires, with false and erased origins, feeding the ambient fears of not only the characters but also the audience, sitting in the dark theater, identifying in complex ways with the story, temporarily relieved by their own experience of dread.

I N HER POEM, "NO SKY," ETEL ADNAN WRITES, "NIGHT'S arrival / in the middle of the dream / cuts life in / pieces." It's never possible to know the middle while inside it, only afterwards, when you find out how much was left, like it often isn't possible to recognize a dream while having one. Night and day divide up time when used as measurements, a record of loss. The disruption of night-fall in the dream Adnan describes might create a rupture in part because it unsettles the timeless space of dreaming, enforcing the temporal linearity that cuts down life. The next line of the poem is "Power accelerates / death." What is the connection here between power's acceleration and night's arrival? I try to think of all the ways state pow-er abbreviated the lives and accelerated the deaths of the sleeping refugees, but there are so many, stretching across lifetimes, creating a string of waking nightmares, many holes in the world.

THE FIRST TSAI MING-LIANG FILM I SAW WAS *I Don't Want to Sleep Alone*. A literal translation of the title would be *Black Eye*. This was around the same time I saw *Mauvais Sang*, in a little self-curated series of movies that approached themes of sickness and contagion that I would watch in bed at night, their uncanny images and cyclical narrative structures reflected on my glasses, my glasses reflected on my dirty computer screen.

A scavenged mattress on which many have already dreamt and will yet dream is at the center of *I Don't Want to Sleep Alone*, as a thick smog settles over Kuala Lumpur. Rawang, a Bangladeshi migrant worker played by Norman Atun, is dragging the mattress home with his friends when he sees a severely injured man in the street, played by Tsai's frequent collaborator, Lee Kang-sheng. Rawang and his friends carry the man on the mattress like a sleeping prince home from battle, and Rawang gently nurses him. Once he is strong enough, the man (referred to in the credits simply as Homeless Guy) begins exploring the streets at night, having sexual encounters, eventually meeting a maid, played by Chen Shiang-chyi, who is cruelly mistreated by her employers, and with whom he begins to fall in love. But by this point, Rawang loves him too, and when one day Rawang returns home to find not only his beloved departed, but the mattress gone as well, his jealousy consumes him. He finds the man and threatens to kill him with the lid from a tin can. They just stare at each other for a while in their violent embrace. Rawang's rage cannot sustain itself against the depth of his love. He lowers the can, his beloved wipes away his tears. There's nothing to say, they understand everything. In the final, dreamlike image of the film, Rawang, his beloved, and his beloved's beloved are sleeping in a row on the mattress. It's no longer in Rawang's attic squat, and now floats on the surface of dark water pooled in an abandoned construction site where throughout the film various rendezvous have occurred. Their breath softly bounces from one neck to the next, rings in a chain, beads on a string. Finally they are alone together in another world where they can dream. They dream of each other. Like angels they recede.

I N THE MORNING AT HER BRIGHT BLUE TABLE MY friend recounts last night's dreams for me. I am thrilled—she's always been a formidable dreamer. She said in one she knew she was dreaming because her grandfather suddenly appeared before her as a young man. I've read that to test whether or not you are dreaming you should flip a light switch and see what happens, as if our minds aren't powerful enough to generate functional dream electricity, when they can create tunnels that never end, children who are not our own but for whom we are nevertheless responsible, lives not ours that we now must somehow survive. The question occasionally arises, *am I dreaming?*, another way of saying, *is this really happening?*, often in reference to uncertainty around not just the reality of a given situation or proposition, but also around how to even go about testing its reality, or verifying its truth claims. In The Bangles 1988 single, "Eternal Flame," Susanna Hoffs asks of the eponymous flame, "Do you feel the same? Am I only dreaming?" As if the way to confirm the truth of a sense or a sensation is to confirm that it's shared, like the transformation of a secret into a confidence, an intimacy. Do you feel that? Or am I only dreaming? Another way to ask the question might be, *am I crazy?* Madness and dreaming do seem to interweave, madness like a sort of dream, dreaming a sort of madness. Are you seeing what I'm seeing? Did you feel it, too?

31

S OMETIMES BRUCE SPRINGSTEEN'S THE RIVER" GETS stuck in my head for weeks at a time. The song is about the death of love, the death of a future, the end of something worth living for, the only future that matters, which is to say one wherein we are all free from the pressure to sell our labor to live and to get married to avoid a consuming shame. Like Susanna Hoffs he poses a question, asking, "Is a dream a lie that don't come true, or is it something worse?" What is worse than a lie? A death? When I don't get the things I want, the things I dream about, I worry that it's because I didn't want them enough, like I can't trust my own measure of my own feeling. I worry that people are always doing what they want to do, really, regardless of any complaints to the contrary, caught in perpetual traps of their own devising. I worry I both overestimate and misunderstand my powerlessness. I want to go to the river too, I want to rest on the banks for a while. I mean forever. But then that's when I understand the river as freedom, it could just as easily be madness or death.

MY SISTER WENT TO LOS ANGELES AND GOT ME an autographed *Hellraiser* poster. It's the best gift I've ever received. Ashley Laurence, who stars in the first several of the franchise as our young heroic final girl Kirsty Cotton, wrote "Laura, much love, Ashley." I consider the possibility that Ashley does indeed love me, that unlike the parasocial love of dreams—where my mind constructs an entire narrative without the active involvement of any of the players, or even my own conscious desires and preferences, since lucid dreaming remains unavailable to me—Ashley and I can love each other without ever speaking or meeting, connected by what? A shared joy in an erotic 1980s nightmare of longing and punishment? Commitment to a certain style of cultural artifact in a way that becomes personality-defining? The poster was a housewarming present. I had spent the day in a truck with a friend and all of my belongings, moving across Brooklyn consumed in a dumb August haze over body and spirit. My friend explained that lately his life has felt like a dream, but neither in a dream-come-true way, nor in a waking nightmare way, but more in the sense that his life lately had moved with the *here I find myself although I don't know how I arrived* sort of motion of dreaming, like the whole world is a pool you can't get out of, your body formless but pruned, weightless as the water you float in, the air cool against your face. As he told me this, I was aware that he had been a real asshole to a number of women in his life lately, and the description he offered of his experience struck me as a kind of excuse for that behavior, but I didn't feel like going there. That night lightning flashed but there was no rain and no thunder. I guess it was from the heat. I felt a great pressure lift and loom and lift and loom all around me, as if at any moment everything might flicker away.

33

I WAS WALKING ON BUSHWICK AVENUE LOOKING AT MY phone when I got tangled in the hanging ribbons of a memorial constructed around scaffolding and a friend texted me that David Berman was dead. "DAVID BER-MAN IS DEAD," he said, which I thought was a weird joke. "Repair is the dream of the broken thing," Berman sang, or still sings whenever I choose to listen, the miracle of recorded sound, always now, always before. So often the truth is not far from a joke. The dream of repair is a joke, everything is broken, what could be more evident? We kiss our friends like our throats are stringed instruments, which is what they are.

I LISTEN TO NOTHING BUT LUCINDA WILLIAMS FOR months. This obsession started one horrible day, or really a regular day after a horrible night, when I heard "I Lost It" for the first time sitting at my desk at work. I left immediately, but of course I came back; it's work. She sings, "I thought I was in heaven, but I was only dreaming," which is so sad. "I thought," being such a sad formation, the uncertain ground of the past betrayed, what you thought you knew, what you thought you saw, that now you see is otherwise. Just before this description she expresses her fear that she might blow away, and that does not sound like heaven necessarily, but does sound like a feeling I was at the time experiencing daily. I mean, what holds anything down, when the stolen ground of this earth and the metaphoric ground of ourselves are both so unstable, precarious? Is heaven anything more than a dream? But dreams are dreams, for one thing, because of their impermanence, their irreality, whereas if heaven is real it is certainly forever, that's part of its whole appeal. There is no end in heaven. Would that a dream could last so long. Perhaps that is what death, madness, love will be. I mean endless. My dreams, instead, are mostly followed by mornings, mornings that are followed by days that are sometimes already ruined by the night before or my own bad attitude. Every day is a new day I tell myself, my new life has already started I tell myself, it's all here, and I'm here too, right where I need to be, which is all over the place. In recent mornings I have looked out windows to the excessive green of Tennessee leaves, the gravel and stones of Tucson yards, the cold tall trees of California, the wrought iron fire escapes of New York. There is no getting "away from it all," it's all always there, I mean where is it supposed to go? That was a real wake-up call, I thought, rushing out the door. The difference between "I have nowhere to go" and "I have nowhere to be but here." In dreams you are where you are, no explanation is required, which is good because no explanation is possible.

36

"I WAS DREAMING WHEN I WROTE THIS, FORGIVE ME IF I go astray," sings Prince, astray being the general direction of all dreams, maybe all things sooner or later. I was not dreaming when I wrote this, or what I mean is I was awake in the night in a strange room, but yes of course I was dreaming, I mean I was swimming in fantasies, as I always am. About movement and summer and a beauty so great in its face the world cannot possibly go on, a weight so heavy it holds me in place, this place, a soft comedown and long night measured in sidereal time and the crystal laughter of strangers, about the sway of velvet curtains lightly brushed by nervous fingers, about life in the mountains, life in the desert, life at the edge of living. If you fall asleep on a train, who knows where you will wake up. Well, you do. If you bought the ticket, that's how trains work. What you will find when you get there, who I will be, and what difference any of it will make, that's all more of the mystery.

THE DIFFERENCE BETWEEN DREAMING YOUR LIFE away and dreaming your way into a new life, a new world. Are both equally possible? But then what kind of limit is possibility in the space of a dream? In dreams I walk with you. Dream lover come and rescue me. Dream lover where are you. Dream, baby, dream.

II.

Laura's Desires

And what does narrative open up
into, if not human love, called into
existence for the first time.

—BRUCE BOONE
My Walk with Bob

then my heart tells me the way
as there is no way

—SIMONE WHITE
or, on being the other woman

T HE PROBLEM OF BETTE GORDON'S 1983 FILM,
       Variety, is economic. Christine needs
       a job so she can avoid returning
to the phantom Michigan from
which her mother calls. The movie
opens with Christine by a swimming pool,
the water audible but just out of frame,
her hair held by a yellow swim cap.
She turns around, looks at a clock
on the wall, wonders if she has
enough time, how much she should rush,
but then she's already here and so might
as well try. The cruel absurdity of being
anywhere, the persistent absence
of an alternative, the restless water.
She dives in, swims across,

flips over, returns, this time on her
back, her arms complete circles
we can only half see, her thighs break
and restore, break and restore
the surface of the pool. A close-up
of her stomach under her striped red suit.
The way the camera isolates her body
in fragments refracted by the pool's surface
both creates and disrupts the sense of
witnessing a display. Afterwards
in the locker room she asks her friend
for lipstick and disappears, returning
from the wrong direction. We had seen her
before in a mirror, now we see her in
the frame, she moves again and we
get both. If the camera shifted slightly,
it would enter the picture reflected,
and another Christine would appear,
inverted on the lens.

I have never liked
going to the gym with others,
although I really like the gym itself.
It's not a matter of privacy, it's more
because one of the ways my gender
informs my behavior is that I always
feel a host, with duties to attend to

by making my warmth, which is sincere,
more immediately perceptible to others
in a way that might provide some ease
against the strain of being a person
in public, while also appearing
so natural as to hardly register.
It's sometimes fun and other times
exhausting, and so a lot of what I do
I need to do alone, or with someone
who I know wants nothing else.
But Christine, played by Sandy
McLeod, and her friend do want
something from each other,
they want not to be alone in the
brutal early evening, and also
Christine needs a job. Her friend,
Nan, played by Nan Goldin, is trying
to help her in this pursuit, the trap
of labor, the threat of return. Christine
wants to be a writer, but she needs money.
They list out options while pulling on
their sweaters against the thick air,
but nothing is viable, there are no
copy editing gigs, people wait
in line to work at failing
department stores. Finally, Nan,
with great reservation, mentions an

opening at Variety, a Times Square porn
theater. Nan worries Christine is not
the type for it, but Christine is more
worried about her bounced rent check,
and the next scene we see her in
Variety's window box between
the lobby and the street selling
tickets for $2. Variety Photoplays
was a real place, however not in
Times Square—the real Variety
was down on Third Avenue between
13th and 14th Streets, right around
the corner from my job now.
The theater isn't there anymore,
though at first I read the address
wrong and thought of another
theater I have loved a block
further south, where I've stolen
blue slushies after spending
afternoons beneath well-funded
disasters. I'd look out the tall
windows of the vacant second
floor lobby, not yet ready to
leave, thinking about people
and what people might think
about me, snow falling on parked
cars, trash bags tripping aimless

pedestrians. Variety, which operated
from 1897 to 2004, was demolished after
its closure, replaced by a glass high-rise
where life, which once had so richly stained
the seats, is now unimaginable. In 1984,
a year before *Variety*'s general release,
a writer for *Bright Lights Film Journal*
described visiting the theater and finding
the film playing upside down, which
no one in the audience appeared to mind,
searching and stirring around in the dark
from their seats to the lobby to
the bathroom, which was located
at the front of the theater behind
the screen. Upside down the movie
rolled on, flesh-filled and weightless.
The journalist said the walls were nothing
special, but the ceiling was covered
in a beautifully patterned tin that had
somehow lasted all those years as glittering
teeth in the dark. He called it a time
capsule. If movies are attempts
to freeze moments, transforming
events into repeatable, rearrangeable
units, then shouldn't their palaces also
take part in this pursuit? All such efforts
are doomed. I wonder what kind of candy

the workers sold at porn theaters to make
the day more sweet, already good as night.
In *Variety* the movie, there is a soda fountain
but no candy I can recall. Once in youth
a boy poured Diet Coke over his cock so
it would be sweeter when I sucked it. I was
touched by the gesture, if also a bit concerned,
as Coke can be corrosive, but it wasn't there
for long. Eventually everyone needs
a woman to appear at a distance and
burn like science fiction's distant cities,
with medical training and the memory
of six or seven summers on the water,
draped in silver from the hidden
filth of icicles, receiving confession
with a clerk's disinterest, a stingray
on the floor of the ocean, dawn's
hardest blue, walking backwards
from a station fixed by nothing but
the firmament of her anger won
in chaos, to stand in her silence
like a vandal at the crypt, in love
with its marble. We follow Christine
as she becomes increasingly
embedded in the social world
of the theater, moving around
the neighboring bars and adult

bookstores that operate in an economy
driven primarily by sex work. One habit
she develops is to narrate pornographic
scenes in a dispassionate, almost
trance-like state to her boyfriend,
Mark, who cannot hang. In one of my
favorite scenes, they sit in his car,
eating Chinese food with forks
straight from an assortment of
paper cartons. They're talking
about his job, he's a journalist
trying to expose some racketeers
he's become obsessed with, enchanted
by the power he perceives as ill-begotten,
power that he longs to dismantle and,
in so doing, establish new power
for himself. There are noodles
on his face. He explains to his
bored girlfriend that if he has to
disclose his sources, that will be
a whole other story, and Christine repeats
the phrase, "other story, other story," slow
as if she's trying to read a water-damaged sign
from across a dark room. "Other story, other
other story, stories, stories, smooth story,
smooth skin," until eventually the story
becomes a black slip on a woman's body

as she paces before a man in an armchair,
stroking his cock. She gets on her knees,
she kisses him, she pushes him away.
She pulls up her slip, she's down on
all fours, the fabric brushes her breasts
as she breathes. Christine describes
her shoes, her ass, the way she opens
up. Kathy Acker wrote *Variety*'s script,
based on a story by Bette Gordon, and
in the porn monologues in particular
you can really feel her. Christine's boyfriend,
dejected, stares into lo mein, until he can't
take it anymore, he asks if she's okay.
She looks confused, "I'm just trying
to tell you about my life." She wants
to be a writer, she's in her boyfriend's
parked car writing her life. It's interesting,
one big critique of the movie at the time
was that it didn't have enough sex in it,
it wasn't pornographic enough, it was a tease.
This betrays the underlying assumption
that porn has to be visual, something you
watch, and so all the scenes where Christine
narrates erotic encounters are just,
what? Not pornography, or worse,
unsatisfying pornography. It's funny
to me these critics don't recognize

their twin in Mark, sitting there
useless, unwilling or unable to
receive what Christine is offering.
Sometimes I wonder if I even like writing,
it's so difficult, and so rarely do I say what
I mean, but then what's likable about
anything under the patriarchy. Leo Bersani
writes that most people don't really like sex,
even if they still feel the need to have it.
Bersani was making this argument from
the same deadly 1980s as *Variety*, in an
essay examining the anti-sex rhetoric
of the conservative Right, gleeful
conductors of the mass death of the AIDS crisis,
shaking their heads on television as they talked
and didn't talk about anal sex, and also of
the radical feminists of that era, in fervent
crusade against pornography, which to them
was the same as rape, a category under which,
according to their logic of domination, all
fucking fell, as all fucking remained subject
to the tyranny of penetration, its absolute power
turning any cavity into a vacuum, a void.
Of these feminists, Bersani writes,

> Their indictment of sex—their refusal
> to prettify it, to romanticize it, to maintain
> that fucking has anything to do with

community or love—has had the
immensely desirable effect of publicizing,
of lucidly laying out for us, the inestimable
value of sex—at least in certain of its
ineradicable aspects—anticommunal,
antiegalitarian, antinurturing, antiloving.

The problem, according to Bersani, is not
that the self is fucked into annihilation,
nor is it the loss of self-control, of power
over the self and the world beyond the self.
Instead, what needs to be challenged is the
inherent devaluing of powerlessness
on which rests this anti-sex argument.
Let fucking be nonteleological, but if it
must be towards something, then let it be
nothing, not reproduction, not even
orgasm, but the temporary abdication
of the numb despotism of being anyone
at all. I return to this essay often, and try
to imagine the contours of the worlds such
world-ending sex makes possible.
The fantasy of an endless fall, ill at
grace, plants that smell sour as I
ferment myself, hurling chunks of
forest floor into the ambulance like,
"First just let me gather a few of my things."
When I think about what it means to me

to be contained in the category of women,
I think first about penetration, which is not
to suggest that this is the unifying experience
of this category, or that this is an experience
exclusive to this category, or that this category
exists beyond its imposition. Not an origin
of anything. Just the most important part
to me. By which perhaps I simply mean
my favorite. Very early in our relationship,
Morgan and I went camping. A friend
had asked me to give a reading in a trolley
adjacent to an experimental music festival,
headlined by artists I was mostly unfamiliar
with, since I pretty much just listen to pop
music and rap. A friend or two advised me
not to bring him on this trip, not to take
things too fast. I was experiencing a period
in my life where I found myself the recipient
of a lot of advice, which I appreciated, as
I appreciate any gesture of love, but
nevertheless consistently ignored
so I could instead be gilded
by an internal trail of chaos. It wasn't
that I thought I knew better, I was
very aware that I didn't know anything,
but my behavior remained just outside
of my conscious control, and I kept

making choices I found surprising,
as if my agency had an agency of its own.
It wasn't a dissociated feeling of watching
from a distance my own actions, but it did
have certain qualities similar to being
a viewer, curious to see what events might
unfold, without any particular predictions.
I wish I could say it was a form of nonattachment,
since I aspire to that kind of openness, but
desire animated every move I stumbled
through, a diffuse and cloudy light. So
Morgan rented a car and we went camping.
It felt like a teenager's fantasy of adulthood's
promised liberties, without the drag
of adulthood's disappointing
responsibilities. The day after
the reading, we drove to a trailhead.
It wasn't so much hiking as walking
slowly across something comparable
to mud, but more buoyant, like a pile
of moss blankets on the softest part
of the earth's belly, so that with
every step I felt both sucked down
and repelled away. Suspended. I guess
it was a marsh? I felt my legs' effort
to carry my weight and a simultaneous
lightness. The trail culminated in a

lighthouse, and when we made it,
we saw that it didn't have a tower,
such as is commonly associated with
lighthouses, but it did have the other parts—
the house, a very bright bulb. We looked
at the water and took a picture together
that I sent to my mom. On the walk back
to the car, the water had risen, approaching
closer to our path, and the sky had gotten
farther away. Often when we have sex
I sense that I am of the same material
as the earth on that day, like the handprint
left on the mattress in an ad for memory foam
just before it slowly disappears, as if instead
of being subject to the force of gravity,
I am its very center, the wet dirt
holding all the weight there is
to hold in a precarious balance.
A lot of singers compare
pussies to lakes, which is apt, not
just for the wetness, but for the
liveliness of lakes, so mysterious,
delicate, overwhelming. The seam
on God's wallet, asleep on the couch
and dreaming an apocalypse with
the volume of snow. It is not possible
to be at home in this world, and there's

nowhere else to go. Is there any joy but
in the ardent exercise of futility? Well yes,
there's poetry, there's making friends,
watching movies, sex, but that's all part
of the same practiced impermanence.
Haunted by a spectral goodness, like
goodness will feed you if you're trying
to be fed. It was formed from the start
in proximity to you, the fountain
the architect dreamed, the children
used to organize the hierarchy
of longing in the tumult of
their callous society. It's the same
as peeling without puncturing
stone fruits or nightshades. We rushed
to the ending and found it abandoned,
but as though disuse were the aim
all along. I remember being a little
drunk in the rented car, Morgan
driving us back from the trolley
to the tent. I insisted on listening
to *Car Wheels on a Gravel Road*
since we were at that moment
driving on a gravel road. Every
thought or feeling I ever had converged
into a single moment, which is true
for all moments, but mostly I forget

or fail to notice. Last month I received
as a gift a plastic blue bird feeder
that I hung on the fire escape. I worry
it might irritate our downstairs neighbors,
precipitating as it does such a fresh
magnitude of shit on not only our own
fire escape but on those below as well,
but then again our neighbors are polite
ex-Texans who haven't complained before
when we've been disruptive, and I hope
won't start complaining now. Yesterday
there was another gathering, mostly
of house sparrows and house finches,
proclaiming at the feeder while I sat
idly by, not writing, not dying. I looked
away, I looked back, and my small
companions had been replaced
by an American kestrel. I felt afraid,
awed by its quiet, and also concerned
that it would drop half the sparrow
it was tearing apart onto the fire escape
below. If it did, would I text my neighbors?
Just hope they wouldn't notice the carnage?
I wondered if maybe this meant
I should remove the feeder, worrying
that I had inadvertently created a trap,
but then isn't that always the risk

of homemaking? The kestrel was
relaxed, the stripes on its back
barely moving. I tried not to watch.
What remains is a hard beak
on the wrought iron, gently unsettling
me as I sit at my desk and try to write
about what I've seen and other things
beyond my power to control or explain
or understand. The presence of hawks
in our dreams is divine. It heralds
freedom and foreshadows loss, also a kind
of freedom. I have sometimes seen hawks
in times of great emotional activity, because
often when I'm happy or when I'm crying
I go to parks so I may be or do so near
a crowd, which is also where city birds of prey
go to hunt. Pretend not to, but watch me
with your watery, public eyes. One difference
between voyeurism and fetishistic scopophilia
is that the former requires a narrative
with subjects and objects acting and being
acted upon, and in this way is always
approaching sadism. The voyeur's
discovery unravels a mystery about the
behaviors of others, and the resolution to
any mystery includes someone's punishment,
the guilty party exposed, the secrets

of strangers flooded in stage light. Scopophilia,
however, does not require, and in fact cannot
sustain, narrative. Pleasure in looking disrupts
the coherence of a story, an identity, and instead
you are left with a face, a neck, breasts, thighs,
and in or from these disentangled parts,
you have everything. Like narrative,
however, this fragmentation is its own
violence, a different loss, the body ripped
apart for or by the viewer. Hated, feared,
adored. I learn this by reading Laura Mulvey,
tired in a museum on vacation years ago,
sitting on a bench surrounded
by ancient sculptures, familiarizing
myself with the concept of "the male gaze,"
which I imagined as a jewelry box, the kind
that plays music when you open it, and
the music is traditional narrative cinema,
and the ballerina that mechanically spins
is a woman's body, caught on film,
and the box is otherwise empty,
too small to hold anything except
one eye, my mouth, a fragment of
my face in its little oval mirror,
ringed in gold.

At the theater, Christine
meets a man, Louie. She finds his apparent
ease—his casual lack of discomfort around
the circumstances of their flirtation
at a porn theater—sexy, and also his suit
and the top of his bald head. She thinks
he's never been ashamed unless he wanted
to be. The first time I watched *Variety* I didn't
totally see his appeal, but then afterwards
I looked at Nan Goldin's photographs from
the set, and it seems like she saw it, because
in her pictures of him I get it, his hot balance
between curiosity and indifference, and the next
time I watched the movie, I was like yeah, okay.
Christine is taking a break, she's going into
the theater for the first time, her ridiculous
ponytail bouncing behind her as she climbs
the stairs, her face reflected in a mirror
near the top. She looks in the projection
booth for a moment but not long, it's a cave
where only moans echo. She goes back
to the lobby and buys a Coke, which she
immediately spills, feeling a little flustered,
feeling a lot of things. This is when Louie
walks over, he's bought her a replacement soda,
she looks at him as she takes a small, slow sip.
Later as he's leaving he stops at her window,

we see him directly and her face reflected
in the glass between them as if she's a shirt
he's wearing. He says he'd like to
buy her a real drink sometime, but
she says she couldn't do that.
In this part of the fantasy that is
her life as she is writing it, it's still
prologue. She knows the one thing
you don't want to do with pleasure
is to rush it, unless that's your thing.
Later, on the street, she sees him
up to some shady shit, another big
part of his appeal, and follows him
into Pussycat Girls Show Center.
Inside we find the cross-class contact
Delany praised, a market and social matrix
disrupted by her appearance as a living,
curious woman. She explores a bit, looks
at some magazines, the men look at her,
but Louie has disappeared. She goes back
across the street to the theater only to
find him there waiting for her. "I just
saw you over there," she says. "I was
hoping you'd get here soon," he interrupts,
"I'm in a rush and I wanted to talk to you."
"Talk to me?" she asks, pointing to her heart
beneath her black jacket, "About what?"

61

He has seats for a Yankees game tonight,
he thought she might like to join. She
hasn't seen a game since she was a kid.
Overhead the sun is bright but not
warm. "A car will pick you up at six,"
he says, and then he's gone,
a busy criminal, and she climbs
back into her little vitrine, imitating
the hot arrogance of his goodbye,
"The car will be here at six."
And then it is six, Christine is in
the car, swept across the FDR, along
the river, their awkward conversation,
predictably about work. He asks if she's
nervous, she says she is. It isn't a problem.
He tells her not to worry and she wonders
if he's asking her to trust him. Perhaps
by way of answering, or perhaps to avoid
an answer, he says curiosity made him
approach her. She blushes, "I noticed you
looking at me." But right now in the car,
they are not looking at each other
at all, they speak side by side with eyes
fixed on the road ahead, as if trying
to memorize the route should they
need to return in a hurry, taking
turns with oblique glances. They are

too close to look at each other at
the same time. The driver, however,
their witness, our twin, observes
everything from the front seat,
his eyes visible in the mirror. The driver
moves the scene, literally, but being
at work, his is an adulterated power,
the power of a viewer who takes
what they can get. Louie asks Christine
if she watches any of the porn they play
at her theater. She says no, but she's
making an unstated distinction
between watching and seeing,
since by now we've watched her
on multiple breaks, stealing inside
the theater, turning her face toward
the screen but her eyes down.
She glimpses a gloved hand
on an ass, and that's enough
for now, she returns to the lobby.
She doesn't tell Louie about that.
She asks him for porn recommendations,
and he says the next time he's there
she should take a longer break
and join him. She makes a joke
about hand jobs—"You have first hand
experience." The date is going well.

He's glad she isn't feeling so
nervous anymore. She wonders
if she's finally being who she
wants to be. The moon over the
half-empty stadium is an eraser
in the sky as the players stand
on the field for the recorded
anthem. Flags dangle from batons.
With more space now, Louie stares
at Christine. Her attention enfolds
his gaze, herself as observed,
the scene. Their figures are backlit
by the green of the field. It almost
looks like rear projection, too bright
to be real, an illusion, Bette Gordon
later explained, she was delighted by.
Drinking her white wine, Christine
is thinking about what will happen
later. In the car Louie had asked her
if she has a boyfriend, and she told him
no. What makes a boyfriend anyway.
But then the inevitable disruption,
narrative's requisite delay, Louie's driver
re-emerges, no longer our voyeuristic
co-conspirator, now a barrier
to our satisfaction as he whispers
in Louie's ear, who then turns

to Christine to tell her something
has come up and now he has to go,
but the car will come back for her
later. It's October, the play-offs,
the crowd shouts at the batter.
"Fuck this," thinks Christine,
as she hurries from the box seats.
She gets in a cab, leans back
and closes her eyes, flushed
from exertion. "Follow that car,"
she says, but we can't hear the words,
we just see her mouth move and her
arm extend, the movie more noir
by the minute, the night more endless,
the sex deferred and permeating
everything. For the rest of the film,
Christine follows Louie in his nefarious
labors. Sometimes I am overwhelmed
by knowing that I don't actually
like or want a thing, I mean not
in itself, I just like and want
the associations, the formative
memories and arbitrary experiences
that, for me, anything I like or want
has come to signify. The kind of movies
I like to watch, the ways I like to have sex,
the food I prefer to eat, none of these

65

things are about themselves, or about
me, not exactly, but the things they
remind me of or symbolize for me,
consciously or not. I mean it doesn't
matter, I know, it's not like there is some
essence beyond context and relation that
should fill the content of my desire, but
then when I think about how my desire is
so essential to the shape of my context,
all my relating, it's like the absolute power
of chance confounds me. I grew up
a believer, splashing around in the pool
of God's omnipotent omnibenevolence,
singing about the font of blessings,
asking it to bind my heart, secure
in the warmed and softened
predetermination of "God has a plan
for your life." I gave up this belief
in an adolescent fit of rage and
sadness precipitated by the
startling and banal realization that
an all good, all powerful, all knowing
God cannot exist in a world consumed
by violence, war, oppression, and cruelty,
because if he knows about all of this
terror and does nothing to stop it,
then he can't possibly be all good,

or even marginally good, really.
My personal faith crisis, I recall,
started when I began feeling
incredible sympathy for Judas
and the excess of his eternal
punishment, and then escalated
as my friends and I began experiencing
predictable small-town bullying for our
social and sexual deviancy, and reached
a climax when my Young Life
minister said I shouldn't keep listening
to Elton John, who was going to Hell.
While my psychic break-up with Jesus
was dramatic, final, totally devastating,
it took me a long time to disentangle
my thinking from the faith that
"everything happens for a reason."
I remember the evening I realized that
this really wasn't true, couldn't be,
not even in a vague, good-feeling,
soft metaphysics way. By then I was
an undergraduate, I was reading a lot
of analytic philosophy, and my cousin
had just died. I was alone in my
apartment on Fulton Street,
my roommates having returned
to family homes for the weekend.

I was lying on my stupid little
twin bed pressed flush with my
window. It was late, and I heard
what could only be the sound
of hooves trotting along
the pavement. I looked out,
and there she was, a lone rider
on horseback, traveling the quiet
Thursday road past my room.
I watched her disappear, and
thought about how everything
that could happen does happen,
in some possible world, of which
this particular world is just one
unexceptional example, and if
everything happens, how can
anything be said to happen
for a reason. It's just that it could
happen and so it did, and I just happen
to be in the version of the world where
this thing transpired, the consequences
of which resulted in my particular
desires and proclivities, my fears,
my fantasies, my understanding
of love and home, what I do, the sum
of who I am. Nothing had to be this
way. I suppose this understanding

could have made me feel untethered
and free, and eventually it did
approach that sense of possibility,
but in registering that the world
could be any way, and here it is,
this awful way, I initially felt more
trapped than I ever had before.
It didn't have to be like this.
Later I came to think about reason
and inevitability and chance differently,
but that night I was inconsolable,
the rider already miles away. Eating cake
with our hands or putting a bandaged
finger in your mouth. So often
I fantasize myself into the lives
of women I see in passing, I could
be wearing her skirt, crossing
her street, parking her car,
feeding her kids, I think. I don't
need narrative to begin identifying,
I will weave my own with the most
exiguous visual evidence, a glance.
I'm interested in *Variety* for the way
it renders the disintegration/evolution
of Christine's conception and
representation of herself, the
transformation she must author

so that her fantasy life and her lived
experience can connect and propel
each other, becoming a kind of
ouroboros of longing that is
fulfilled by the pleasure of
longing. Or it isn't even really
a transformation, I don't think
Christine necessarily changes
over the course of the movie, but
rather what was already true surfaces,
we recognize it was always the pool
she was swimming in, she's been
our comic-sexy hero all along. I am also
interested in *Variety* for what it invites us
to reflect on when we think about self-
representation and identity-construction
for the women who made the movie:
Bette Gordon, Kathy Acker, Nan Goldin,
and Sandy McLeod. In a 1982 interview
between Bette and her friend and
collaborator Karyn Kay that they
conducted for a series in *BOMB* called
"Women Looking at Other Women,"
Karyn says, "I think each of us acts
out these fantasies. It's just fragments.
I think we want to be the women
in our films," to which Bette replies,

"We are." To admit something
is also to claim it, shameless, maybe.
How to want to be the women that
you are, anyone. Like Christine
in the car, like me right now, they
are writing their lives. In some ways
it seems that Sandy, our star, is the
farthest from Christine, in terms of
what biography I can uncover, although
when Kathy first met Sandy on set,
she turned to Bette and whispered,
"She's perfect." This must have
been a small relief, since originally
Kathy wanted the great bodybuilder
Lisa Lyons for the part. It could just
be that Sandy gave the fewest interviews
at the time the film came out, and so
her interior life, or rather the way
she might choose to frame it, is
the most unknown to me, and
thus I assume her to be the least
like Christine. One thing they have
in common is that Sandy and
Christine (and Bette and Nan
and me) moved to New York
for art-reasons and fantasy-reason:
Sandy wanted to be a cinematographer,

but at that time in New York—despite
its retroactive celebration for being
"so collaborative" and "so open"
with the rise of No Wave everything—
it wasn't even possible for her to
get a job loading film. Instead
she became a continuity supervisor,
then called a "script girl." I remember
once sitting in the bedroom of a
continuity supervisor on a summer
afternoon as she described to me
the strange and tedious pressure
of making sure each prop is returned
to its spot, half-filled cup on the table,
shirt righted, and so on, the great effort to
construct the illusion of linearity from
the temporal and social chaos of a film
schedule, a room full of people doing
various things together. How predictable
that this demand for order is, not even
women's work, but girls' work. Telling a story
as a kind of housekeeping, a practice both
welcoming and totally alienating, arbitrary
and naturalized, public and secretive,
hidden in the middle. She was looking
everywhere for other jobs, but I haven't
seen her in a while and don't know how

that worked out. Sandy was not especially
an actor when she took the role, and she
hasn't been in much else, although she has
continued to live her life in the industry.
In 2014 she made her first feature film,
a documentary about a Norwegian seed bank.
I listen to interview after interview to see
if she might say something about *Variety*,
but instead she just tells the same stories
of agriculture and Norway and fate—
the serendipitous moment of meeting
her subject over breakfast; walking
on a night so dark and cold that she felt
afraid, her face nearly frozen by the wind.
It's cool that she's focused on her new stuff,
she sounds very fulfilled by it, and I'm
left to wonder, as is my tendency, how
she got the part of Christine, why she
wanted it. Maybe the thing she had
most in common with Christine is
just that she needed a job. Nan and
Bette I know were already friends
before filming began, they met
on the phone when Bette was still
living in the Midwest. A mutual friend
was visiting and staying at Bette's place
while Nan stayed at his loft back in the city.

But his lock was fucked up, trapping Nan
inside the apartment, who then had to
call Bette, who called someone who
called someone else who came and
broke Nan out, and that is exactly
the kind of thing I expect to happen
when I'm housesitting for friends,
with all our busted apartment doors.
Nan and Bette grew close after
Bette moved East and got involved
in the storied downtown experimental
art scene. Nan Goldin the photographer
and Nan the character in *Variety* are so
similar as to be almost indistinguishable,
they even work at the same bar,
Tin Pan Alley, have the same friends
who hang out there, talking about
the same things. The appearance here
of transparency, the apparent relationship
of identity, where Nan is Nan and
none other, feels to me fitting
of her artistic ethos, thinking about
the way she positioned her photos as
her visual diary unveiled, more than
documentation of her relationships,
but the relationships directly, not
mediated by the camera but

rather clarified through the
image-making process,
an offering to the viewer of
her eyes, her face, her feelings,
her voice in our heads, her shared
memories suffusing our own like
a color. In addition to acting
in *Variety*, or maybe better to say
appearing in it, Nan worked as the
on-set photographer, and she incorporated
two of the images from *Variety*'s set into
her enormously important book, *The Ballad
of Sexual Dependency*. The first
is of Sandy in the ticket box, the other
of her friend, the radiant Cookie Mueller,
pictured during her appearance as one
of the women at Tin Pan Alley, hanging
out, talking about men and work.
There are photos from other film sets
too, and in fact one of those photos,
of Vivienne Dick in a green dress
on the set of another Bette Gordon
short, *Empty Suitcases*, is also
visible as set decoration in Christine's
room, the one she can't afford.
Seeing these portraits of characters
next to portraits of people, marked

particularly by their sense of vulnerable
immediacy, as if truly exposed, too bright
to be unreal, I get a sort of tumbling
feeling, art and life as railroad
apartment where you have to pass
people sleeping when you get up
at night to pee. Since *The Ballad*
is presented as "directly from my life,"
the inclusion of these photos from movies
raises exciting questions about what
"from" and "my" and "life" can mean,
as James Crump also points out in
his afterword for *Variety: Photographs*,
a monograph that came out in 2009.
In the set photos, for example,
the portrait of Cookie might be
a portrait of Cookie, it's just
captioned, "Cookie at Tin Pan
Alley, New York City, 1983,"
but Sandy is being Christine,
who is no one, who is a story
that Bette and Kathy wrote
together. Or maybe it's between
takes? When do I ever stop
being myself? Where do I go
when I'm putting on a show?
When I'm not performing?

A few weeks ago in one of the
more elaborately organized group
sex experiences of my life, there
was a moment where I was on the floor
of an apartment in North Brooklyn
watching a friend fuck her girlfriend.
As the latter got closer and closer
to coming, I felt myself fade further
and further from her awareness, she
needed to concentrate, to be alone
with her concentration and her
girlfriend's hand, a throne. At the
same time, I felt myself become
more and more central to my friend's
conscious awareness and experience,
I felt her watching me watch her
girlfriend's transforming face,
and so I performed my watching, my
pleasure in looking, which was easy.
Or maybe I was projecting on the
orgasming girlfriend, her perceived
departure from the room something I
imagined because that's what it's like
for me, that I want to feel observed
until I'm ready to disappear, and to
disappear I close my eyes, I'm all
feeling in darkness, slick fingers inside

me, wet tongue in my ass, all eyes
on me finding my way to an expanse,
a descent, an escape, release, whatever.
"Can I come?" "No, not yet," "No,
not yet," and then eventually, "Yes,
now." In her introduction to *The Ballad*,
a totally beautiful piece of writing,
Nan explains,

> We all tell stories which are versions
> of history—memorized, encapsulated,
> repeatable and safe. Real memory,
> which these pictures trigger, is an
> invocation of the color, smell, sound,
> and physical presence, the density and
> flavor of life. Memory allows for
> an endless flow of connections.
> Stories can be rewritten, memory
> can't. If each picture is a story, then
> the accumulation of these pictures
> comes closer to the experience
> of memory, a story without end.

Like, I assume, most people, my memories
are totally untrustworthy, I keep them
in the same place I keep my fantasies
and they start to smell the same. Did I
really see a lone figure on horseback
on Fulton Street at midnight, or did I just

imagine her? Did I conjure her, create her,
channel her, witness her, project onto her,
misunderstand her, all because in that
moment of loss, I needed her? I don't
super care one way or another,
although for some stories, I do
understand it's important that
they're true. In that same intro,
Nan explains that she photographs
because—

> I don't ever want to be susceptible
> to anyone else's version of my
> history. I don't ever want to lose
> the real memory of anyone
> again.

I know that's not why I write, or
I don't think so, I'm just trying
to think some things through, but
perhaps that's just because from my
particular subject position I'm less
susceptible to anyone telling
my story for me. When I see
Nan Goldin's pictures, I think
they show the kind of nonnormative,
potentially (and sometimes actually)
dangerous desire that both the conservative

Right and anti-porn feminists were
so worried about, they show a world
of sex that makes and unmakes
subjecthood, and more than sex,
abuse, friendship, love—all those
dependencies. All the people in
the photos look so fucking cool.
Or maybe I don't completely relate
to Nan's explanation of her
artistic practice because I don't
relate to having a version of my
history that isn't an amalgamation
of other people's versions of it. Or,
I just said that, but I wonder if
in some way in gesturing towards
this network of relationality I'm just
trying to distance myself from how
undeniable my own lived experience is
as an organizing principle, the incredible
force of my unique, often myopic,
perceptions, because I want always
to escape myself, feeling as I do
overwhelmed, embarrassed, kinda
fucked up, and honestly not that
comforted by the knowledge that
you probably feel the same way too.
I don't know, I don't want to

glory in my fantasy of a self,
but pretending this self doesn't
exist isn't helping me much either.
Years after her death, I remember
finding a picture of my cousin
getting ready for her wedding,
a guerilla-style affair in a gazebo
at the West Des Moines Botanic Gardens,
the cold days of early spring, 2002,
performed quickly and unofficially
by my family before we could be
asked to leave. In the picture she's
sitting on the floor, looking in a mirror
leaned up against her bedroom wall,
applying mascara. Visible in the corner
is my fourth grade photo, framed.
Seeing this, I am so moved I almost
laugh, this surprising recognition,
evidence of the relevance of our
love on our daily lives, a background
on which other stories unfolded.
I retrieve this photo from another
family guerilla intervention, twenty years
later in Colorado where we gathered
to surreptitiously bury the ashes of
my aunt and uncle, my cousin's mother
and step-father, in a public park, a plan

that, to be honest, I was against, but I
didn't say anything because I didn't want
to bring more stress to an already
stressful situation, and anyway I do
think my aunt at least would have
found it funny. Sometime between
the Iowa wedding and the Colorado
funeral, my mom spoke with a psychic
she sometimes visited in Northern California,
and afterwards she called me from a sunny
parking lot to say that Joan, the psychic,
told her that my cousin watches over
my sister and I, that she's with us all
the time. Joan said that she was never
meant to have a long life, but now
she protects ours. She makes sure
I avoid situations I only think I would
want but would later come to regret.
I collapsed on the sticky fake tiles
of my kitchen floor, I couldn't breathe,
but in a good way, no news had ever
brought such relief. I was surprised
by the intensity of my reaction, since I both
miss my cousin terribly and also feel sort
of strange about it, because at the time
of her death we had grown apart. I was
living in New York and she in Iowa, I

almost 20 and she almost 30, I focused
on my own shit, and she focused on hers.
When I learned that she died, I didn't know
what to do, I took a shower and listened to
"The Way You Look Tonight," a song
I can't imagine that she liked, one that
I had barely thought about before
that moment, but suddenly it reminded
me of her beautiful face, the way she
would show up to church in scandalous
dresses and laugh at everyone over
donated pastries. Looking back on
this wave of relief I felt at the psychic's
reassurance, I wonder how something
as platitudinous as "she wasn't meant to
live a long life," could have comforted me
so deeply, since haven't I been on this
whole long trip about how nothing is meant
to be anything? I don't know, my cousin
is with me, she loves me, she forgives me
for everything, she's a slow shimmering
comet, she controls the radio to send
messages when she wants to, she's free.
Let it be so. Nan Goldin first showed
the photos that would eventually
comprise *The Ballad* as a slideshow
at Mudd Club and later OP Screening Room,

sometimes with music to heighten
the sense of the cinematic, sometimes
with Dean Martin's "Memories Are
Made of This." This play with earnest
vulnerability and a kind of sentimentality
that in its excess sounds at least a little
sarcastic feels like more splashing
in the bathwater between life-
and myth-making. But maybe I am
only projecting sarcasm, I mean, that
really is what memories are made of,
did I learn nothing from crying in
the shower to the promise, "someday,
when I'm awfully low, when the world
is cold, I will get a glow just thinking
of you"? Night skyline from the bridge
on a stalled train, what water carries
below, tunnels I've also sat in. Dark
night in Colorado smoking with
my surviving cousins, now well
into our adult lives. Hard nights
in North Brooklyn, feigning aimless,
Billie Eilish. Back in the desert night,
the first time in eight years,
kissing an old friend in front
of a new friend's small apartment
complex, the creosote smell,

questionable ethics. Long nights
near the Northern border,
listening to soundtracks on a
tape player, safe but not feeling
that way. Drunk and willful in a tent
at night at the end of a gravel road,
hopelessly in love. California pre-night,
my parents go to bed at nine, apologize
for it, a few miles away there's a beach
called a morgue, empty. At a gas station
under a half-moon, not yet a nonsmoker,
not yet a lot of things. I think sometimes
it's best not to overthink the things
that make you feel alive, not to worry
so much if there is something wrong
with the objects of your devotions, but
instead to see what it might mean to
follow them without apology or fear.
If you can do so without causing
harm, or with the intention not to,
it's hard. If in so doing you can be
more free. If you can take anyone
there with you. But when have I ever
had a thought or feeling and not
worried it from every angle I could
conceive. To my surprise and basically
against my will, my interests are growing

increasingly spiritual as I get older,
having thought I renounced all that,
but now instead of the relief of certainty,
I think it's the generalized erotic satisfaction
of knowing that I don't understand shit,
not anything, and should not ever
expect to, that draws me to
spiritual reflection. Also I find
I take more and different risks now,
since I've discovered that for the
most part, I would rather have the
things I want than be afraid
of them, or that the fear was part
of it all along, not a problem to
solve. I also take more naked
pictures, looking more now for
what is there than what is missing.
Some possible young Christines:
Christine is active in a number
of extracurriculars, but prefers
dance to them all. The sound
of plastic soles on the polished gym
floor, rolling shorts once at the waist
to make them shorter, maybe twice.
Or Christine looks forward all week
to Wednesdays and Young Life.
Every sermon sparks in her an

urgency. She lifts her voice in song
but she can also feel it dropping
down, her voice in her stomach,
tickling her hips. She is filled
with grace. Or Christine cultivates
her reputation like a vine on brick.
Rumors make her feel important
and so does making people cum
and so does lying alone
on her stomach in the grass
and seeing a fast-moving shadow
pass overhead but not seeing the shape
that cast it. I'm one of those people
with a lifelong weird fixation on
Wittgenstein, I think for reasons
having to do with how particularly
emotional his style of analytic
philosophy is, how desperate
it often feels. It's very relatable.
Wittgenstein asked again and
again what it means to be certain,
what it means to have doubt. What can
be said to exist beyond a conceivable
doubt? Is it possible to doubt whether
or not you have been to the moon, or if
your hand is where you perceive it to be?
I notice Morgan and I use the word "know"

differently, he says you can't know a thing
unless it's true, what you are doing in that
case is believing, thinking, or imagining.
I don't think you can ever know whether
or not something is true, so it's possible
to know something and be wrong about it,
and discover this mistake only later, if
at all. Either because you changed, or
the thing you knew did. Wittgenstein writes,

> 'I know where I am feeling pain,'
> 'I know that I feel it *here*' is as
> wrong as 'I know that I am in
> pain.' But 'I know where you
> touched my arm' is right.

I think one thing he might mean
is that knowing is relational, possible
only because of a net of other things,
the fire below the ground below
the fire. Other arms are how
you know your arm. I'm not sure
if this is true, Elaine Scarry argues
the opposite, the problem
of the mystery of other bodies
and their conditions, pain the only
certainty, and then only for the one
in it, the one undeniable thing. The trouble

I am concerned with is not so much
the specific content of anyone's doubt,
not necessarily, unless it pertains
to anyone else's deservingness of
and capacity to be free, but instead
I'm interested in the temptation
to place a negative value on doubt
as a state, a way of being and relating,
like a value judgment on powerlessness.
I'm thinking about a doubt directed
toward the logical and necessary
inevitability, the obviousness,
of anything, replacing all
confidence about the stability and
identity of any event or person or
ambient mass of consciousness with
the awareness that they will surprise
you. You will meet yourself, you will
meet your world, you will meet the day
for the first time, every time. You will not
figure anything out. I think there's
something particularly pleasing about
Morgan and I having different relationships
to the possibility of knowledge, since
so much of what is interesting to me
about knowledge has to do with love.
I can be in the presence of love

when I can stay with all the things
I can't know: the uncertain future,
the truth of anyone else's heart,
what anyone else's orgasm feels
like in their body. The gratitude I feel
for these mysteries, even in the moments
when I sort of wish I could resolve them,
gives me the incredible courage
necessary to love. Beginning
at the belly until it reaches the portico.
The whole reason for resting, the only
way to have the energy to do a thing
after work. Here's the cargo of many
wishful flotillas, veins on a thigh,
a little blood on the pillow. Overpowering
incense before the early drive home.
Considering all the places I've never been,
Jackson, Vancouver, a barn party, the heel
of a flood, it's a rare kind of marble to
be here, thanks. It's harder to imagine
Christine in old age, in part because
I have received less cultural material
narrativizing the emotional and sexual lives
of older and old women. I like to imagine
I will think less and less of myself
as a separate and self-contained thing,
that I will become more messy and

harder to define. I like to imagine
that for Christine too. And to
imagine that the more anyone
explores the disordered contours of
their desires across the course of their
erotic life, by which I mean the whole
of their life really, the more rich and
disorderly those desires will become,
so the sex you have the farther you get
from youth is the most weird, the most
fulfilling. I suspect this to be the truth, but
since it's less marketable, being more
about giving away than purchasing,
it is less often represented in popular
narrative art and portraiture.
It's my birthday, I wake up and clean
cat shit off the wall, how did it even
get there, go out to refill the birdseed,
fantasize myself the mother of winter,
listening to children argue about character
in the backseat of a car I'm cautiously
driving across slush. Turning an orange
this way and that across the counter.
I text my friend I am grateful
for the cat shit's reminder that
I am blessed to live in service,
which is true, another mostly futile

practice that is the only available
relief from the agony of having
been born. In the lobby of Variety
there's a poster for a movie called
Laura's Desires. Much later, after
the movie has unexpectedly become
a part of my life and personality, I learn
that Bette included the poster as a prop
in homage to Laura Mulvey, to whom,
she explained, the whole movie is
a love letter. I'm not thinking
about Laura Mulvey when I see
the poster, I'm thinking about how
I'm going to write that poem,
and it'll be about me and my desires,
my alienation from my desires,
my attempts to fulfill them, both
successful and failed. *Laura's Desires*
is from Germany, originally called
Laura's Gelüste, which at first
I misread "geslüte," meaning "blossom,"
and before that "geslute," which means
nothing in German but "slut" in Afrikaans.
I don't speak German, but basically
I understand the film to be about Laura,
who is sitting at the beach, dreaming
of a vacation to Hamburg where she

has sex under a variety of circumstances
with a number of people. The movie
takes place almost entirely within this
narrative frame, and I suspect
that if I understood the language
I could more easily discern if she were
reminiscing or envisioning to fill
the space of her beach day. In this dream
space, whose arrival is signified by
a sort of cloudy white visual transition,
Laura is delivered directly from the airport
to a sexy photo shoot, where she watches
another woman dressed in diamond-studded
lingerie, posing for a camera with a phallic
tube light she gazes at in astonished wonder
and then puts between her legs like she's
about to fly away. Laura can't believe
her luck, as soft blurring around
the edge of the frame again signals
the start of fantasy, now within fantasy.
Laura is on top of this diamond woman,
a necklace hanging from her neck,
tracing a silver message across
the woman's breasts while they kiss.
Soon they are both naked, except for
their necklaces, and Laura is between
the woman's legs, elated, and then

the fantasy ends, as does the photoshoot,
and Laura greets her friend, the photographer.
She follows the model to her dressing room
where she finds her smoking at a vanity.
Laura sits between the mirror and the model,
next to lipstick tubes and tissues, they kiss.
She goes on to have sex on a variety
of 1970s leather couches, in small airplanes,
cars, at dinner parties—basically she has
a great vacation. The Hamburg dream passage
of the movie ends with a naked woman
delivering a tray of orange juice to guests
after an orgy. The camera zooms in between
the glasses and onto her breasts, getting closer
and closer until it's no longer possible to
recognize the image beyond soft tones
of orange and peach, dissolving back
to the shore where Laura is dressed
in white, walking into the sunset like a
bride but alone, wondering where she
goes from here. I wasn't named Laura
for any particular reason beyond my mom's
fondness for the name, which is cool, I like
fondness. At times I have been intensely
obsessed with *Twin Peaks*, which I think
has something to do with the pleasure
of hearing the name Laura repeated

with such frequency, but also more
to do with the ways Laura Palmer
provided me the teenage girl version
of Christ that I needed when I needed
something Christ-like to believe in, but
that thing couldn't be Jesus, and also
couldn't be myself, and something as
vague as "art" just wasn't going to
do the job. I know Lynch's portrayal
of Laura has been criticized as
fetishizing a dead girl, romanticizing
and obscuring the reality of the
violent precarity of girls' lives, and
as a fan of the show, I have found it
really meaningful to contend with
this critique. It reminds me in some
ways of perhaps the most important,
or certainly the most useful consequence
of the anti-porn, sex-negative feminists
we've been talking about, which was
to insist in their argument that
sexual violence against women
and girls—it perhaps goes without
saying that in this intervention
they completely excluded
trans women—was not rare
and exceptional, in the way it had

been previously represented by both
Freud and conservative fantasies of
"family," but in fact happened every day,
all the time. Demanding a confrontation
with this brutal reality, transforming it
from open secret to public knowledge,
has had a lot of consequences, some
of which have protected survivors of
sexual violence, and many of which have
not protected anyone at all, but only
created the possibility of further
surveillance, policing, and violence.
In the fictional case of Laura Palmer,
I think it's not her powerlessness
against her abuser that makes her
such a striking character, one that
transformed not only the lives of everyone
in her town within the universe of the show,
but also inspired the vast and devoted fandom
that envelopes *Twin Peaks* in the universe
I'm writing from. Just speaking for myself,
it's the undeniability of her power that
attracts me to her, the way she burns
through her town, in danger and dangerous,
her desire her crown, making a truth
very obvious, even if her neighbors
refuse to see it. She's totally radiant.

It's complicated. When we see her
in dreams, speaking backwards,
we know she knows everything
already, while we're out here
with the useless law, looking
for clues. And there's Petrarch,
of course, creating a whole cosmology
and poetic form for a Laura who he saw
some Good Friday from a distance,
and then obsessed over for the rest
of his life, "haunting Laura in church
and on her walks." No one now
is certain who his Laura really was,
if she really was, if her name was
really Laura, which is unsurprising,
since she's both hyper-documented
and totally effaced, not a person
but a vision of imagined love.
She might have been Laura de Noves,
the "virtuous wife" of Count Hugues
de Sade, ancestor to the Marquis.
The style of writing Petrarch created
to describe his desire for Laura, famously
composing in Italian vernacular so he could
really tell the people about his longing,
is called "Cathexis." It refers to the
concentration of intense mental energy

on a single person, a fixation on
the regenerative force of desire,
here endlessly renewable because
endlessly deferred, perfect and undying
on the page smudged with oil from
Petrarch's humanist fingers. I don't
know if we can really think of these
as seduction poems—which are more
like speech acts attempting to
precipitate an event, to enact a
transformation in the world, to get
the lady to descend from her tower
and fool around in the forest of being
young and in love—because rather than
some unfortunate and hopefully temporary
delay, here it seems the fact of being
unrequited is intrinsic to Petrarch's desire.
Longing is itself the longed after event.
Petrarch doesn't just write about Laura,
he writes about air that touches her,
ground that shifts beneath her, projecting
himself into the rocks she stomps across
in a semi-passive obsession fulfilled by fantasy
alone, content to look a little, imagine
a lot. Through his cathexis, all of this energy
is concentrated in a single vehicle, and yet
the vehicle itself is ultimately irrelevant,

more anonymous than a theater balcony
hookup, because while a blow job might
be delivered by anyone, the singularity
of their spit and throat and tongue and lips
makes theirs for a moment the only mouth
in the world. They are the only one they
could be. But in Petrarch's sonnets, there is
no specific material embodiment around
which his dreams coalesce, even temporarily.
Outside of his poems his Laura doesn't
exist. That consummation was not
the point seems all the more likely
given that the poems continue long after
Laura's death, extending his idealization
of her ever more easily because now she is
even farther away. This is another difference
from Laura Palmer, whose haunting feels
incredibly active to me, she becomes
clearer and clearer, filling her Pacific
Northwestern sky, temporarily halting
local industry, transforming the social
and erotic lives of both friends and
strangers, not exactly an avenging
angel, but not not that either, or even
more, a diarist. We don't know
how Laura de Noves, or whoever
she was, felt about being a muse,

although I think we can guess
she felt somewhere in the range
of annoyed to terrified, but then I mean
maybe adoration from a distance was
her thing. I hope so.

When Bette Gordon
moved from Wisconsin to New York she
had already been making movies.
Avant-garde and structuralist, they
often involved complex technical conceits,
copying and stretching and splicing frames,
expanding and contracting seconds
of motion. To someone like me,
someone whose taste has been
severely impacted, arguably damaged
by the technicolor candy of pop music
and Hollywood movies, a lot of this
early work is pretty boring. She got here
in 1980, I think, with her then-husband
and collaborator, James Benning.
My favorite movie they made together
was in 1974, *I-94*. Still certainly anti-narrative,
it was more sexy, confrontational but in a
very emotional way. James and Bette
set-up a camera in the center of train tracks
at the bottom of a kind of ditch beneath

two unadorned overpasses, with long yellow
grass reaching drily on either side. There
they took turns filming each other. Bette
filmed James walking from the middle distance
forward, in a straight line along the tracks,
towards the camera, his white skin and 1970s
hair sort of yellow in the sun, the brown
island of his pubic hair. James then filmed
Bette, or I'm not sure what order they did
this in, beginning at the camera, the lines
of her shoulders and then her waist then
her ass almost filling the frame, walking away
along the tracks. Each frame then alternates
between either Bette or James, giving the
appearance almost of a double exposure,
each a ghost to the other, their paths
overlaid, as if they were walking towards
each other when instead they were each
walking alone. Whenever I pause
the three or so minute video, one figure
disappears, leaving the other unaccompanied
on the small screen of my laptop at night.
The audio functions similarly, they are both
recorded monologuing, and in the beginning,
when Bette is closer, her audio is also louder,
and then following the moment where their
bodies seem to meet, impossibly for a second

appearing to occupy the same exact place,
James's voice begins to supersede hers.
Bette is describing how frustrating it is,
how she's trying to get a job but no one
takes her seriously because she's a woman
and, as she explains, "she doesn't try to
make herself ugly," which I experience
as a frustrating bit of internalized misogyny,
even as her broader complaint about
uneven opportunities remains important.
I don't know what James is saying,
even as his volume relentlessly
increases, I'm still trying to make out
phrases of Bette's complaints. She later
explained that their collaboration
can't be extricated from their personal
history, their having fallen in love, and so
their movies are documents of their attempt
to relate to one another, sexually and in other
ways, through the marked difference
of their experiences of embodiment,
of being artists, sexual people, in the
world at all, intersected daily by
complexes of power differently
wielded, often in ways they were only
dimly aware of, when they were
aware of them at all, trying to

figure out how to say what they
wanted to say, which they were also
trying to figure out. By the time they
arrived in New York, things were ending
between them, which was rough, and
as with any significant breakup or love,
their art and lives changed afterwards,
though not in a causal way or anything,
just like, sometimes you need to change
everything for fear that if you don't,
you'll die. Or maybe I'm projecting,
which is a very hard thing to resist
when reading too much about
other people's lives. Now in New York,
Bette got involved with the Collective
for Living Cinema, she met a bunch
of cool people, she felt totally
bewitched by the city, just wandering
around for hours like a kid in an
enchanted forest, not worried
about money. Around this time
she went to The Kitchen to see
Kathy Acker read from *Eden Eden*.
By now she was dating Tim Burns,
and Tim and Kathy had slept together
before Tim and Bette got together—
sorry for being gossipy—and so

upon meeting Kathy, Bette felt
a little jealous, and I imagine it added
a different spark to their first encounter,
already erotically entangled, a sexy
shared knowledge, a feeling at once
intimate, exhilarating, and uncomfortable,
new friends already fluid bonded. Either
then or soon after, they decide to collaborate.
Here comes *Variety*. In her wanderings, Bette
did a lot of what Christine will do in the movie,
transgressing various all male sanctuaries, like
sex stores, porn theaters, the Fulton Street
Fish Market. She described a feeling of
intoxication. When she first saw the shining
marquee of Variety Photoplays, she wanted
to swallow it. She stopped, transfixed, and
she gazed on the sidewalk, her thoughts
stretching out across all the directions
of her life, both planned and unexpected,
or perhaps her thoughts left her completely
and she lost herself in her perception
of light. As she stood there motionless,
the projectionist arrived for his shift,
and seeing her unusual behavior,
asked if she wanted to come in, and
oh my god it's all she ever wanted,
so he showed her around, she wandered

the lobby, paused at the soda fountain,
went to the projection booth and heard
the moaning, saw the skin made
of colored light, expanded like
gods at work. Did she feel something
like belonging? Was she turned on? Did it
seem kind of silly? Did she wonder
what people were so afraid of? By now—
"now" here meaning 1983—her boyfriend
Tim was curating a show at Artists Space
called *Emergency* to address the rapid
disappearance of funding for artists
from the buckling NEA. For the show
he gave a number of filmmakers $75
to make a movie. Bette was one of them,
and she made *Anybody's Woman*,
which ended up being basically
a treatment for *Variety*. It stars her friend
Nancy Reilly as she explores Variety
Photoplays—much the same way
Bette did and Christine would—
and tells pornographic stories to
a disinterested man, one story
in particular Christine will later
repeat to Mark. Almost like a fable
or a dream, this story is of a hitchhiker
who spends a series of nights

at a woman's house. On the first
night, during a fit of sleepless hallway
roaming, he, being unobserved himself,
comes upon the woman lying on a
wooden table. A snake slithers in,
moves over her skin like a cloud
crosses grass, spelling in a strange
language across her breasts and
stomach and thighs, sliding into her
pussy, a single limb, a curving line,
circling her from the inside. On the
second night, once again unable to
sleep, or really he just had better
things to do by this point, the man
witnesses a similar but escalated
scene, the snake replaced by a tiger.
"Who is the woman who lives in this
house?" he wonders, or maybe, "Am I
dreaming?" I don't know what he does
during the day, but the third night
arrives, and finally his host is on top
of him, her hands on his chest, nails
digging in. Spalding Gray also appears
in *Anybody's Woman*, sitting next to
Nancy in an otherwise empty theater,
summarizing pornos he'd seen, markedly
less witchy than the one Nancy offered.

He rates the appearances of the women
performers, explaining a simple economic
relationship where more expensive tickets
meant more desirable bodies. It's obnoxious.
Karyn Kay in a voiceover outlines a scene
from the movie's namesake, Dorothy Azner's
1930 *Anybody's Woman*, in which two heartbroken
millionaires spy on two broke sex workers
through a hotel window, getting ideas.
This collaging of stories, of characters
who speak but don't necessarily become
any more clear through their speech,
who don't evolve over the course
of the film, who remain both unstable
and unchanging, and who, despite all this
the viewer can easily, almost inevitably
relate to, is part of a transition away
from the formal structuralism of Gordon's
early work, into the more narrative,
but still weird, style she would adopt
for the rest of her career. In many ways,
the fact of *Variety*'s shift towards story
was just as controversial as the
central presence of porn to the story,
since to some the presence of linear-ish
narrative felt like a betrayal of both
avant-garde filmmaking principles

and feminist discourse. Alongside
the sex wars, debate around how to
represent women in regular, not necessarily
pornographic movies also got heated
at this time, and one possible answer
that was offered to the problem
of women on film was to reject
narrative entirely. According to
this logic, narrative functions to fix
the objectified image of a woman
within a male fantasy, naturalized
through the illusion of linear time
and continuous space. Liberation
could thus be achieved through
showing the container, exposing
its construction, pulling time
apart, folding and unfolding
space, no beginning, no middle,
no ending, no characters, no plot.
I mean yeah, I won't pretend to deny,
that's pretty appealing, even as I also
can't deny that I love to hear a story,
I love narrative art. Amy Taubin,
one of the only critics who was
into *Variety* upon its initial release,
wrote in her *Village Voice* review,
"Until *Variety*, Bette Gordon was a

nice girl. She made the films she
thought she was supposed to make."
Even though I really admire the way
Taubin praised and uplifted this film
for the decades it was mostly neglected,
a lonely champion for the work until
it finally started getting more attention
in the 2010s, following significant
screenings at Tribeca Film Festival and
a retrospective at Anthology in 2011
(for which Taubin once again offered
her version of the story, "the pressures
of the feminist discourse were such that
Gordon would have to make several
confused efforts at being a 'good girl'
filmmaker before she could cut loose
in her barely disguised autobiography,
Variety"), I still find this "good girl"
framing of her early work sort of
dismissive. I think Gordon really was
trying to figure something out, not
passively rejecting her own desires
in pursuit of cultural or academic
acceptance or recognition, and also
I'm pretty sure Bette consistently saw
herself as a "bad girl," saying specifically
in one interview when asked about

her relationship with Kathy Acker,
"Kathy was a bad girl. I was a bad girl."
But I mean, these are categories I've had
my own fascinated and fucked up
relationship to all my life—just to
be able to write this poem I've had
to actively suspend my conception
of myself as belonging or being
relegated to either group—and so
I sympathize with the swirling canals
of feeling and desire on which float
such overdetermined utterances as
"She was a good girl," "I was a bad girl,"
or (my favorite) "We were bad girls."
After a screening in Berlin of her film
Empty Suitcases, a movie I've never
seen because it's not available for free
on the internet, Bette was offered
$40,000 from a TV station in
West Germany, ZDF, which was
at that time funding a lot of
experimental work with minimal
oversight of the artists. ZDF gave her
the assignment to make a movie about
voyeurism and porn. She combined the
$40,000 with $25,000 from NYSCA,
$15,000 from Britain's Channel 4, and then

an additional $5,000–$10,000 from an
unknown (to me) investor, which I imagine
she secured when ZDF ran out of money
sometime between October 1981 when filming
began and January 1982 when it was restarted.
Funding struggles seem only to have gotten
more pronounced for Bette after *Variety*,
despite the fact that in many ways her feature
debut was a success, that year's sensation
at Cannes. In another *Village Voice* article
championing Gordon in 1998, Amy Taubin
explains that Bette spent years trying
to adapt another film, *Love Me Tender*,
but could never get the money together,
and spent the next many years working
on 30 minute episodes of things for
Showtime and Playboy, before
finally releasing her next feature,
Luminous Motion, fifteen years
after her debut. Given these money
struggles, it surprises me that in so many
more recent interviews Bette complains
about young filmmakers now, "just putting
videos up on YouTube and hoping for
Netflix deals." I mean, whenever
I'm subjected to artists who grew up
creatively and socially in the 1980s

(or the '60s or '70s or '90s) complaining
about artists who are trying to figure out
their thing now, an unfortunately frequent
occurrence in my life, I have this feeling
of trying to look across a chasm of loss,
but the immensity of what's been lost
is so unbearable that it becomes
like a distorted mirror, such that
recognition, not of direct identity
but of similarity, of kinship, becomes
basically impossible, complicated by
resentment, heartbreak, dread.
It's hardly surprising that I find the
closeness of chance and fate
so fascinating, since one rules all
on earth and the other is a trick.
The fact that your name, your birth,
your era, your social position in a global
historical network, are all erratic
turns through unmappable chaos,
that's one thing, and then it's a whole
other story that this is also true for
everyone you love, everything they do.
Revolutionary mystic Simone Weil
describes this, the challenge to know
that love in this world is born of
the most unstable circumstance,

living, and to love inside it nevertheless,
as God would, regardless of love's object
being constitutively arbitrary
and fleeting. She writes,

> The only good which is not subject
> to chance is that which is outside
> the world. The vulnerability of
> precious things is beautiful because
> vulnerability is a mark of existence.
> The destruction of Troy. The fall
> of the petals from fruit trees in blossom.
> To know that what is most precious
> is not rooted in existence—that is
> beautiful. Why? It projects the soul
> beyond time. The woman who wishes
> for a child white as snow and red as
> blood gets it, but she dies and the child
> is given over to a stepmother.

Most people I love, including the dead I've
never met, share a concern for what's outside
the world. For Weil, the mother who dreams
dies, but before she dies she gets everything
she ever wanted, and that doesn't die
with her. We are not infrequently permitted
to glimpse beyond this world from right here,
deep in its stuff, people and plants and animals
holding on, both part of the net and making

the net. The mysticism of bodies mid-cooking,
cleaning toilets, fucking, talking to birds.
I have never known what spirit means,
but I have often wished I could take
breathwork more seriously. I imagine
my breath with the perfection of
serialized narrative, a world sustained
by half its life consuming carbon dioxide
and expelling oxygen, the other surviving
through taking that oxygen and creating
carbon dioxide. Independence is a lie,
I would choke on it. But then whenever
I try to focus on my breath it's like
I forget how, the rate of my inhales
increasing to meet my permanently
elevated heart. Or I just get bored
and start to look at the internet, trying
and failing not to measure myself
against others. A friend and I once
talked about the unparalleled pleasure
of hearing someone say your name
in another room, speaking about you
to someone else. Not overhearing
an entire conversation of which you
are the subject, which I think is
distinctly unpleasurable, just
some small fact stated, like "Oh,

that mug is Laura's." We guessed
that the satisfaction begins in feeling
confirmed in your continued existence
in someone's life even when not literally
in their presence, and somehow knowing
that you live in someone's mind is proof
that you actually live in the world at all.
I remember reading Weil on the train
while moving through a particularly
shattered period of my life. I couldn't
eat anything, could hardly speak, my skin
was so dry everything I touched cut me,
like my body was trying to become
the wound I felt like all the time, and
now whenever I return to my copy
of *Gravity and Grace*, little reddish brown
spots on every page remind me that
I'm alive. Once I was taking the train
to a place I felt really nervous to go,
when another woman got on, also
radiating her anxiety like a halo
of perfume. As if our vulnerability
magnetized us to each other, she sat
by me and we started talking, which,
being a shy and private person, was out
of character for me. She was carrying
a suitcase and dressed like she was

ditching a ball. She told me
her mother had died. I don't think
at the moment I knew where to
begin to tell her that I feared
I was disappearing more with
every breath I took, but I think she
got it anyway. We came as close
to clinging to each other without
touching as was possible across our
warm plastic seats. I do not think
I would recognize her if I saw her
again, but if I hadn't found her
in that moment I know the pressure
hanging over me would surely
have driven me under, eardrums
popping in my skull. Permanence
in intimacy is an unnecessary goal,
since each intimate exchange in some
way forever alters all participants,
regardless of what shapes they go
on to maintain between them.
Lord I know she texts me,
an attic light, a month. The day
we spent chewing flowers
into paste, the city, our love
for it, brushing ashes from
our neighbor's shoulders with

a feather. As brothers then.
At different points in my life,
having my own bedroom
has meant different things to me.
The low-hanging vortex that bumps
against my nightly forehead. Lord
I know she weights me, dropping
each amethyst as a proverb from
her hand. I like your horse,
your earth bed, your dark-eyed
boy, your bottles that glitter
with the sun. You said meet me
at the gate, but gate to where.
Any illusion can undo you if
you want to be undone. An old
dear friend, a thing for which
there are no words. Burning
is one way to clean, yes, but
sometimes a mess is better
or best. Can tears ever truly
be wasted? I mean it's not like
I'm going to run out. In her essay
about making a documentary
on Weil, Fanny Howe describes
the feeling of absurdity in being
anywhere, the requirement to always
be somewhere so long as you live.

Since birds are here, they might as well
sing and fly, since I am here, I might
as well take a long time to process
my feelings and to do so under your
casual gaze, to research movies, as if
in narrative forms I will find
some adequate propitiation.
In 1982, in what must have been
one of its earliest screenings,
Bette Gordon presented *Variety*
at the Barnard Conference on
Sexuality in a workshop entitled,
"Pornography and the Construction
of A Female Subject." Some of the
guiding questions of the infamous
conference—offered in the steering
committee minutes which had been
compiled as part of the *Diary of
a Conference on Sexuality*, a booklet
intended for distribution at the event
but instead confiscated by Barnard
administration the day before—included:

> What does sexuality mean? …
> How do we define it? How can we
> put on a conference, if we haven't
> defined it? Have we approached it
> too narrowly, treating it as a thing
> apart from the whole of women's lives?

and

    Is it possible to have a 'value free'
    space? Can sexuality ever be discussed
    apart from values?

and

    What is the status of pleasure
    in feminist theory and analysis
    and in the social world in which
    women live? What are the obstacles
    to autonomy and pleasure; how do
    women attempt to get pleasure?

and one of my favorites, not from
the official meeting minutes
but a note from one of the committee
members whose handwritten name I
can't decipher,

    Must autonomy and
    nurturance remain split?

The conference, which focused not only
on sexual violence and its consequences
on the lives of women, but also on
sexual pleasure and the conditions
under which it might be attained, radiated

controversy that stretched out in advance
of and well after the event itself, in relation
to the moral debate burning through
feminist discourse around BDSM
and pornography, practices, as you
can probably guess, that were understood
by radical feminists of that era to be
fundamentally misogynistic. A group called
Women Against Pornography, or WAP,
protested the conference, which was
entirely predictable, despite the planning
committee's stated attempts to avoid
making any inevitably controversial
direct statement of values like,
"pornography is good" or,
"pornography is bad." The WAP
protestors wore shirts that read
"For a Feminist Sexuality" on the front
and "Against S/M" on the back.
One of the many problems with
this argument was that "feminist
sexuality" was understood in this totally
essentialist way, as something tender,
loving, gentle, sex on a blanket of flowers
that wouldn't disturb a single petal,
the opposite of the self-annihilating
degradation they perceived in all

penetrative sex, or sex that explored
fantasies of dominance and submission,
with or without penetration, not
understanding that it's precisely
this self-annihilating degradation
that is so fucking hot, and so fucking
helpful to so many people. For a while
over the summer, Morgan and I dated
a woman who is a bit older than us,
she would have been a kid when
Variety came out, and she would
occasionally describe herself as
a "sexually liberated woman."
I hadn't thought about this
particular phrase for so long
before meeting her, or possibly
I had never thought about it at all,
and each time she said it, I felt
completely elated, just thrilled.
Did I also feel sexually liberated?
I don't know exactly, it's more the
language itself I feel moved by.
While it could imply a possible
binary, a before and after, either
sexually liberated or not, instead
I experienced in it an articulation
of straightforward exuberance

121

about the lived possibility of
liberation, or not even possibility,
its reality, however imperfect
and incomplete. She said it
once while we were getting
drinks at her neighborhood bar
across the street from a park
crowded with sun-bathers, the
same park where Morgan and I
first made out several summers
before, and it reminded me
that the feminist lesson about
the personal (that it is political)
remains a daily revolution, one
that can be fun even as it is
totally exhausting and hard too.
I also feel elated when I remember
that at the time of this writing, WAP
does not mean Women Against
Pornography, it means Wet-Ass Pussy,
thanks to the intervention of artists
Megan Thee Stallion and Cardi B.
The summer of its release, their gorgeous
and obscene single "WAP" glazed
the city with its ubiquity, its looped
sample of Frank Ski's 1993 single,
"Whores in This House" echoing

from every car, its litany of directions
on where to spit, swallow, drip, blasting
from every T-Mobile storefront. It's not
like 1982 is pure speculative memory
or anything, it's still present, and so
the response to "WAP" of course also
included some moral terror, even
Snoop Dogg took a break from
filming commercials to say some shit
about a woman's secret Nile jewel,
a remark to which Offset responded
with a reminder that it was a good time
to shut the fuck up. And while I am
charmed by his solid point, it's still
so dumb that Offset had to respond
at all, like Cardi's public permission
to be a slut. Remember when Nicki Minaj's
"Anaconda" came out? Before the video
dropped, feminists on the internet were
so excited about what they perceived as
a reclaiming of the objectification that is the
foundational premise of "Baby Got Back,"
but then when the video was released
suddenly it was like this great betrayal,
like Minaj's language had been okay
but her image could not be, as if her body
and the bodies of the other dancers

were too much, were not right, as if
the representation of their physical
presence, the choreography of both
their desirability and their desire, was
excessive, overwhelming, inappropriate,
unacceptable, bad politics, and Minaj
was accused of reinforcing the objectification
of women by performing and marketing it
herself, a woman. It was, once again,
some white feminist puritanical bullshit.
The impulse to punish and silence
a song or a celebration of desire,
the pleasure of a wet-ass pussy,
having one or eating one or both
or more, remembering that a pussy
can, like sex, be whatever the fuck
you want it to be, is constitutive
to the system of violence against women,
and absolutely not a way out of it.
I don't mean to suggest that all desire
is liberatory, and I too am troubled
by the ways women are expected
to perform their desirability as well
as their desire in public to accumulate
a certain kind of adulterated cultural
power, I just want to offer that
a strong reaction of fear or rage

in response to that performance says
a lot more about the person experiencing
fear and rage than it does about the person
or people or artifact that fear and rage is
directed against, such as Megan argues
so persuasively in her music video for
"Thot Shit." This is part of what, I think,
the Barnard conference was hoping to
address in asking about the status of
pleasure, in asking not just what sexuality
is, but what sex is. I feel a deep appreciation
for the question on the possibility of evading
valuation totally. I mean even here, when
I'm like, what if we stopped devaluing
powerlessness, what if we stopped
devaluing doubt—and by we, I mean,
of course, I—am I not just offering an
alternative model of valuation? What
do I do when I'm not evaluating?
On the car ride back from meeting
Morgan's grandmother, I remember
he and I talked about my anxieties
and fears around being in an
open relationship, my unfortunate
capacity for or even tendency
towards jealousy. Then I was quiet
for a while, passing trees and ditches

and medians, and then we talked about
the possibility of a language that would
emerge singular and specific to each
new encounter, a way to escape
the tyranny of identification through
static categorization, a fundamental
instability that would demand a different
level of collective responsibility for
words, but would also perhaps offer
a transformative liberation of meaning-
making and so also the world, which is
made of meaning. We got candy and
coffee at a rest stop and I felt the hot
possibility of balance between total
resolve and an unfixed and endless
un-resolution. It was early January
and I was so brave, if gasping between
waves can be said to be brave.
I wonder still about this desire
to valorize doubt. Doubt has
this amazing way of tricking
the person holding it into faith
in something else, an underlying
assumption that is the base from which
it's possible to doubt other things.
I mean, think about Descartes,
out here like whatsoever can be

doubted, will be doubted, and then
relying on the most egregious
assumptions about what thinking
means, claiming to upend everything,
but instead replicating and naturalizing
the same dominant structures and
arguing that it all makes sense now.
Fanny Howe writes,

> Doubt has a lot in common
> with infinity, being boundless,
> and the authority of what is
> presented as truthful may be
> more unsettling than what
> remains a conjecture.

And she's such a believer! But she's
a believer in the kind of way that
makes proof impossible, undesirable,
outside the world of meaningful referents.
I wonder if doubting is something I can
barely even do, a precarious suspension
I can only maintain in fleeting starts, since
it pushes me outside of the words available
to describe the things I'm so sure of, even
if it's negative certainty like, knowing
when something is definitely *not* true,
so that more than a concept, doubt

is a feeling, past a vague, "I wonder if it
shouldn't be this way," and more towards,
"Maybe it isn't this way at all." But for
this sort of utopian doubt I fantasize,
by far my more daily experience
of unbelieving doesn't tend
towards a metaphysical longing
to exceed the traps of language,
but instead towards a constant
hum of self-doubt, taking its
place in the top five organizing
frames through which I experience
my life. It is at times for me an agony
to make any decision, when every possible
outcome seems equally ambiguous
and present, regardless of my small
interventions, so how can I
write this email, prepare and eat
this soup? Perhaps it makes me
uniquely tedious to love or work with,
since sooner or later I'll be collecting
your input on everything. I'm sure
in part this impulse comes from my
internalized understanding that
my life is irrevocably entangled
with everyone I've ever met and
never met, and so the consequences

of my actions will have an impact
beyond what I can know, and as
such, I have a responsibility to try
and not fuck anything up too much.
But then isn't this incapacitation its own
form of fucking up? The underlying belief
this doubt betrays is that I have no idea
what I'm doing or what any of it might
mean, and as such I am easily swept
into other people's versions of events
if they demonstrate the slightest confidence
that they know what's going on. I think this
is part of why Nan Goldin's promise that
in her photographs, she's offering the
reality of her subjective experience is
both thrilling and overwhelming to me,
because I'm like, "Wait, you know?"
I wonder what I would be like if instead
of doubting any decision I make, I doubted
my social training that I am incomplete
and incompetent, that I can't be trusted,
that I need someone to tell me what to do.
This is part of what I'm trying to work out
in the poems I write, the sex I have,
the spiritual practices I'm attempting to
develop. What if instead of writing
Laura's Desires, I wrote *Laura's Doubts*?

Would that be the same book? Maybe,
but it would be a different porno. Maybe.
When Kathy Acker agreed to write
Variety, it was after *Great Expectations*
and before *Blood and Guts in High School*.
She had already been around the experimental
performance and filmmaking scenes since
her early teenage years, but she had never
written a script before. Bette offered her
the story she had already written,
the story that traced some of her
own experiences exploring Variety, and
Kathy expanded it, drafting dialogue,
adding scenes, suggesting possible
visual or stylistic choices. Mostly Bette
used everything Kathy gave her, with the
exception of a more explicit sex scene
between Christine and Mark, a second date
between Christine and Louie, and a fourth
porn recitation. Now, I am not really
a researcher, I learned all this
because a scholar at Queens College,
Kevin L. Ferguson, accessed Kathy's
papers in the David M. Rubenstein Rare Book
and Manuscript Library at Duke University
and then wrote a paper I found online in
which he details what he found there in two

documents: "Kathy's Changes to Film" and "Additions to Dialogue for *Variety*." This is also how I learned about the funding sources and filming timeline, much gratitude to you, Kevin, may our paths cross one day.

He notes that the word "desire" comes up twenty-two times across the sixty-six pages, and offers the following examples I will reproduce here:

> "We start with Christine. . . .Because it's herself her desires which are awakening."

> "As all desire must happen at NIGHT because NIGHT hides our fears."

> "Every step forward in desire, remember, needs two backward and around steps."

> "Reality or appearances are a mirror of desire. Desire involves collusion."

> "This is desire: following after, the play of presence and absence."

> "This language is desire not communication unless you too are (as are the audience ((we hope)) [sic] in the world of desire."

> "Christine moves as straight ahead toward her goal, desire, as the train."

"This will is what is not but will be,
is looking, thus the nature of desire."

The vision of animating, propulsive desire
that Acker here offers thrills me, where
Christine's pursuit of Louie, steady
as the train tracks down which Bette
and her lover once recorded each other
walking, is also her pursuit of her own
transformation, her becoming,
in itself also a kind of destruction,
an escape, and also neither transformation
nor destruction, but rather an unveiling
of what was there all along, obscured
by shame and social pressure.
The distinction Kathy makes about
the language of desire as a world you
need to enter into before you can
read it or speak it reminds me of
something else I love in Nan's intro
to *The Ballad of Sexual Dependency*,
when she argues that sex isn't so
much a performance as a way of
communicating something that can't
be communicated any other way,
which is like, maybe a bit idealized,
but nevertheless I think true,

sometimes, and very hot. I love too
Kathy's understanding of desire as
occluded, unclear, willful and
wandering, a place where certainty
and uncertainty are not at odds,
but exist in fruitful tension under
the sweet and emboldening dark
of night. I write this whole long poem
about me and my desires, and my
expectation in so doing is that
I will come closer to understanding
them, to knowing them, what they
actually are. My perfect plan is foiled
by the inscrutable nature of the experience
of having a self. Nothing is clarified
for me, I continue to want nameless
things, things with names that seem wrong,
things I don't want to want, things
I'm afraid of that nevertheless when
I manage to fulfill make me feel like
an electrified current for days on end,
until that feeling fades too. I contemplate
writing this poem again, but this time
showing it to no one, ever, and in that
space of secrecy's abandon, finally
arriving at a kind of truth. But then
that was basically my plan this

first time, and yet instead of hiding
this poem, to my surprise I couldn't
stop reading it to people, emphatically,
every chance I got. And for me
the pleasure of secrets anyway,
is that they occur in a realm
that is neither true nor untrue,
since they can't be evaluated
by comparing the utterance to
the event it attempts to describe,
as there is no utterance, and possibly
no event either, no thing to point to.
If I have a crush on a friend,
for example, but I know I don't
stand a chance with them so I
carefully hide it, I don't tell
anyone, does the crush obtain
existence, so to speak, or does
it hover somewhere undisclosed,
unverifiable, unreal? You're probably
like, Laura, of course it exists, secret
crushes are real things, constitutive
and common elements of social life,
like secret wishes, secret fears, these
are experiences, and experiences,
when in the midst of one are
totally undeniable, even if no one

else knows. Just because it's easy
to lie about it doesn't make it any
less true. Yeah okay, maybe.
*Laura's Desires II: Each Time
It's Personal. Laura's Desires II:
The Realization of That Fantasy
Was Different From What I Had
Expected It to Be Like, Gosh.*
I listen to a dharma talk by
Geoffrey Shugen Arnold, Roshi,
the abbot of Zen Mountain Monastery
in the Mountains and Rivers Order,
and he says something that really
helps me. I'm still struggling with
my meditation practice, so I listen to
these recordings while I run in circles
around Owl's Head Park, a hill that
overlooks Staten Island and a waste
treatment facility that in the summer
overwhelms the park with the sour-
sweet smell of decay. With my senses
thus overwhelmed I can finally quiet,
temporarily, my attention. Shugen Roshi
is talking about attachment and nonattachment,
and he draws a distinction between
expectation and intention, or aspiration.
With the former, there is a clear picture

of the thing desired. Like, "If I do this,
I will receive this, and it will make me
feel like this, and be perceived
in this way," and "this" could be
love, fame, money, whatever.
With the latter, there is no image to hold
in mind, because there is no concept
to attach to, nothing to organize
language around. It's not about
manifesting some vision,
there can be no vision, no goal.
Instead, I intend to be compassionate,
wise, and free, but I don't know what
any of that would look like, even as
it's already true, not some possible
alternate to the person I am, but what
and who I am, fundamentally. What
a relief, to recognize in this unfixed
uncertainty not a failure, not an obstacle,
and not a success either, but something
deeper than success or failure, outside of
those categories, of any categories.
So then, for example, when in
a conversation with someone
who uses the shield of "being
pragmatic" or "being realistic"
to argue that it isn't possible to

return the land, or to abolish the
prisons, or to organize resources
such that no one has to sell their
labor and the planet isn't rapidly
dying because "how would that
even work?" or "what would that
even look like?" I am not forfeiting
my argument when I admit that
I don't really know. This lack
of knowledge is no problem,
presents no hindrance to living in
or into the world I desire, but
instead is the only way to
get there, to already be there.
I mean, maybe this explanation
will not be the most persuasive
to the imaginary pragmatist
I'm rehearsing a debate with
here, but I don't know, maybe
it will, and at least it will help
me to feel less naive, less defeated,
less confused. And in a smaller way,
I don't know what forms my own
life will take, even as I attempt to
form it around the things I care
about and believe in. I don't know
how it will look, will I get better

and better at addressing the challenges
of being in an open relationship,
will I find ways to live that are less
atomized, will I stay in New York
even as it becomes increasingly
impossible to live here, will I
be guided by love and compassion
in all my thought, speech, and action,
as is my intention, I have no idea,
but this presents no problem, it is how
it needs to be in order for me to be
open enough that love and compassion
can guide me through. Everything
is fine. I must be stress-crying
for some other reason.
Shugen Roshi ends the talk with a poem:

> And then right and wrong ended
> standing alone on Earth
> there is no beaten track

Hearing this, the grass of the park
opened up and swallowed me, the sky
overhead opened up and swallowed me,
the already hot morning opened up
and swallowed me and I said,
"Oh my fucking god, finally."
Making the calendar for the seashell

hospital, the embroidered tulip on
the comforter getting crusty with
age. First I had to gather the women
to finish the mural, applying blades
of grass with old mascara combs.
Ruby bra strap next to ribbed
tank top on the candidate's sloping
shoulders. In every corner, a barely
domesticated animal. I've planned
so many activities for our day.
The last time I was lonely was
the last time I'll be lonely.
The question from the conference,
"Must autonomy and nurturance
remain split?" runs through my head,
like a better way of asking about
the whole Madonna/whore thing.
There is no way to be autonomous,
to be free, without everyone else
also being free. Care and freedom
go together; liberation and vulnerability;
accountability and sex. It is all too
connected to be divided into parts.
This is a thing we already know,
in the erotic knowledge ever-present
in our bodies way of knowing. It's this
knowledge that demands we ask

for more for ourselves, for everyone.
As Audre Lorde writes in "Uses
of the Erotic," an essay without
which this poem could not exist
because of how deeply it changed
the way I think, the words I have:

> The dichotomy between the spiritual
> and the political is also false, resulting
> from an incomplete attention to our
> erotic knowledge. For the bridge
> which connects them is formed
> by the erotic—the sensual—
> those physical, emotional,
> and psychic expressions of what
> is deepest and strongest and
> richest within each of us,
> being shared: the passions
> of love, in its deepest
> meanings.

The separation of autonomy and
nurturance is another violently
enforced binary, that, as with all
binaries, has no existence before its
enforcement. Anyone who lives
a day, a moment, outside these
binaries is themself the bridge
that we are told is impossible,

doesn't exist. Weil says when
you love someone perfectly,
you don't want anything from
them, just for them to exist. A love
like God or a mother or a
lover endlessly chill. Do I want
things from the ones I love?
Oh my god, yes, of course I do,
I'm here on earth, about to burst
I want so much. I want my love,
my loves, to end the world, but to
love me first, and to reassure me
of this constantly through nice
texts, occasional physical affection,
and regular attention. Mostly I just
want everyone to be free, which
feels silly to say, like I'm being
too earnest, a level of earnest that
then comes across as either
childish or insincere, but I don't
know, here we are. I asked what
I want, now I'm telling you.
At the end of *Variety*, Christine
has stalked Louie all over the city,
including a scene where she breaks
into his room at the Flamingo Hotel
in Ashbury Park and goes through

141

his suitcase, touching his clothes,
his lighter, his porn, traced by
the pink neon of the sign outside.
It is the culminating sex scene
of the movie. She steals his magazine,
Tiny Tits and Cute Asses and falls
asleep next to it, sweetly. It's like in
Otto Preminger's *Laura*, the part
where it's gradually revealed
that the detective who was assigned
to investigate the murder of Laura Hunt
has, despite having never met Laura
in life, fallen in love with her memory
as its been delivered to him by her
many surviving admirers and then
augmented by his lonely fantasy. He's taken
to haunting her abandoned apartment
at night, touching her furniture, drinking
her liquor, and then in the film's famous
twist (sorry if you haven't seen it), Laura
returns, opening her own door, disrupting
his dream of his perfect dead girlfriend,
so much better than he could have
imagined. It's a wild movie. One
version of a summary for *Variety*
might say it's a movie about a woman
who becomes increasingly unable

to distinguish between her fantasy
life and her actual life, a woman
who loses it. In another summary
we might say it's a movie about
a woman who gradually and then rapidly
transforms her actual life into a fantasy.
Or we might say it's about a woman
becoming herself. We might resist
the pressure to summarize at all.
In the final ten minutes, Christine
dresses in lingerie and puts her hair
in a ponytail, displaying her body
to her own gaze in a set of mirrors.
She's redecorated her apartment,
the poster for *Laura's Desires* is now
hanging in her room, the elliptical promise
of its tagline "… always become her reality"
a kind of motivational reminder, her own
"hang in there." She's become unreliable
at work, stopped returning calls from
her mother, from Mark, even from Nan.
She watches porn at the theater but
psychically collages it with a fantasy
of herself and Louie back in the motel room,
together this time, moving slowly,
doing almost nothing at all. Two women
kiss in front of a fire. Christine's face

fills the screen, expectant. Louie
is looking at her, he's taking off
his tie. Arriving at the film's climax,
Christine calls Louie and tells him
that she's been following him. "I know
what you've been doing." We can't
hear his response. You remember
the mystery of the racketeers Mark
was so invested in? Christine has
solved it, maybe, or maybe
those are two unrelated plotlines,
either way she doesn't even care,
she's not interested in revelation
or redemption or justice, she's not
trying to clarify anything, not trying
to accumulate facts, she's not interested
in coherence. She says she's not sure yet
in answer to some question, I imagine
along the lines of, "What do you want?"
She tells him to meet her at Fulton
and South Street, from her reaction
we perceive that he agrees. *Variety* ends
on a shot of the intersection, empty
but for the vastness of all potential
for anything in the quivering void,
the rise of John Lurie's score
replacing all diegetic sound. Reading

Gordon's presentation from the
Barnard conference, I am disappointed
and surprised when she explains the
conclusion we are meant to draw
from the empty intersection is that
Christine didn't show and neither did
Louie, that the emptiness is meant
to deliver the movie's moral argument
that pornography cannot fulfill
the desire it either produces or
merely encourages, because looking
will never be touching, fantasy
will never be enough. I know it's
her movie, but this is my poem,
and I am not convinced. I wonder
if, in the swirl of many controversies,
maybe at that moment Gordon felt
a pressure to take a definitive stance
in describing her movie that otherwise
resists such transparent messaging.
In later interviews Gordon drastically
walks back that tidy symbolic translation
of the final shot, offering instead more
space for ambiguity, indeterminacy,
narrative opening. This is much closer
to what I experience looking at the vacant
intersection, the streetlight illuminating

nothing but the silent cobblestones. I feel
I am being asked to not know, and to deal
with that unknowing, to just stand there
at the empty corner, surrounded by night.
Maybe the meeting had already happened
and now the lovers are on their way to
the rich eroticism of a motel still
in the early days of its grand decay,
where they will pass back and forth
a power between them, lush and rank
like any other bodily fluid. Maybe
they are still arriving, maybe
their arrival is endlessly deferred
and that deferral is precisely the source
of their pleasure. I prefer so much the relief
of not knowing, the permission it offers
to create my own fantasy of their encounter,
temporary and subversive as a song
that makes some people rich and
some people free. I think authorial intent
is far from the last word in anything,
despite what I just said about this
being my poem. I mean it's my
poem for me, my poem to you,
you're going to do with it what you're
going to do with it, just as there's nothing
finally stopping me from having it just

the way I want it, filmy and mysterious,
a floral shirt in a window, watching myself
crossing a street, knowing and not knowing
where I'm headed, not hesitating, guided
by an intuition of the palace where
a bag of candy melts and reconstitutes
itself in breath glittering in the dark
of an incidental space. Outside there's
the weather, moods, imaginary money.
People with varying degrees of skill
as storytellers, who want different things
for their lives from their lovers.
Things that come and go. A friend
reads an early draft of this poem,
and offers gently that in the end,
she feels no closer to understanding
what I mean when I refer to "freedom,"
despite it appearing as such a central figure
in the poem. Sometimes I think all
clarity is an accident, stumbling
into a description or explanation
of something I hadn't previously
understood, and maybe still don't,
and for a moment language somehow
coalesced into a window, a mirror,
a camera, a door. In which case I have
equal control over moments of obscurity

and lucidity, which is to say, no control.
This would be a convenient way to
avoid saying what I mean. It helps
sometimes to question it out, like,
"does freedom feel like anything
else?", "is freedom an absence or a
presence?" I read about a debate
between Neoplatonic Christians,
arguing either for God's omnipotent,
omniscient, omnipresent omnibenevolence—
the positivists' claim that so fucked
up my youth—or for God's complete
unknowability, such that anything
that could be said of God would necessarily
be untrue because nothing true about God
could be sayable. I'm afraid I'm explaining
this negative epistemology incorrectly,
because I've just said something
about God, so it must also be untrue.
Freedom, I am convinced, is a presence,
as Ruth Wilson Gilmore explains,
it is a place. What makes something
a place? Relative proximity and distance
to other places, having a history, a population,
mostly belonging and fantasy, I think.
Not a nihilistic gambler's freedom of
having nothing to lose, which in my

experience is more like a panicky trapped
thrashing feeling, but instead a freedom
of living within and helping to maintain
structures wherein it is possible to do
whatever it is you find yourself called
to do. Swim, marry, divorce, be responsible
for a boat, look out a window, stage a play,
abort a fetus, express your gender, feed
your friends. As an aside in *On Certainty*,
Wittgenstein expresses regret for all
the confusion apparent in his writing,
but in that regret a hope that future readers,
in meeting the questions he swung
his arms towards again and again,
might find something to hold. You see?
He always said the most romantic things.
I wonder about the nervousness
I have felt and still feel around writing
about the actual sex I actually have.
I sometimes find it hard to be in
the place where sex and words meet,
or rather I love to be there, but find
it hard to get there, sometimes.
It helps to slow down and ask,
"What do you want, Laura?" And
then I can't stop. I want to be
sucked under a current, or no,

to float, or no, I want to be cast
in your elaborate fantasy but to
have a clear enough role that
improvisation is easy. I want to feel you
from inside, to tuck your hair behind
your ear, to have known you when we
were children, our arms wrapped round
our knees in the back of a parked RV,
to taste your molars, be your optional
pendant, but also to never speak to
you again, because wanting reminds
me of the control I lack, a seance
in an infinity pool, a poem I continue
to write even when I feel I'd like
to be done. I'm crossing the bridge
on the way home from work. It's dark
out, the Verizon sign over Lower
Manhattan glowers. Across from me
on the train an older woman chews
her gum with such commitment to
the mechanics of her jaw moving
it's confrontational. I want to watch
her, and I think she wants to be watched
by anyone, but I know that if we act
on these impulses we will both be
ashamed and potentially react to that
shame differently, so instead I read

the advertisements and imagine taking
her place. St John's, Education That
Elevates. La Mujer del Diablo, Vix
Original. Book Your Party At
Race Play More. Something for
discount scrubs I can't quite see.
I do want to tell you things as I know
I love to be told. If I thinly veil my
autobiography, will it be easier to speak
freely? If I wrote *Sarah's Desires*?
Night is a panel she folds back.
She transfers from train to ferry.
She turns around, calls her love
her lovebug, simmers and elects,
a mysterious partisan opening
a door. Once I was in a friend's car
driving towards the sunset,
to a movie theater built over
a demolished amusement park.
It had been a local controversy,
years before we got there,
though we were still familiar
with its basic shape. The sun directed
rays straight through the windshield,
four lanes eclipsed in its glare.

ACKNOWLEDGMENTS

Thank you to The Poetry Project, site of my ongoing poetic education, spring of all my closest friendships, my family home. Thank you to Stacy Szymaszek, Simone White, Nicole Wallace, Will Farris, Kyle Dacuyan, Kay Gabriel, Anna Cataldo, Roberto Montes, Sasha Banks, and Andrea Abi-Karam. Thank you Eileen Myles. Thank you to every person in every feminist reading group I've ever been in. Thank you Rachel James and Anna Gurton-Wachter. Thank you to all my teachers. Thank you Anselm Berrigan, Elaine Kahn, Ben Fama, Jackie Wang, Jacqueline Waters, and Wayne Koestenbaum (with whom I first began writing "Dream Dream Dream"). Thank you to Brandon Brown, who helped me so crucially with this book as both inspiration and editor. Thank you to Nightboat, to Lina Bergamini, Lindsey Boldt, Jaye Elizabeth Elijah, Gia Gonzales, Trisha Low, Stephen Motika, Kit Schluter, and to Caelan Ernest Nardone. I wish for every poet the experience of working with an editor as thoughtful, inspired, generous, fun, and kind as Caelan. This book, like all books, is made possible by the existence of many other books by many other writers, quite a few of whom have already been named on this list. To name a few more— thank you to Dana Ward, thank you to Akilah Oliver, thank you to Fanny Howe, thank you to Susie Timmons, thank you John Yau. Thank you Bernadette Mayer. Thank you Anne Boyer. Thank you Ry Dunn and Rebecca Teich. Thank you Benjamin Krusling. Thank you Ted Dodson. Thank you Dave Morse. Thank you Anahit Gulian. Thank you Adrian Shirk and Amber Lewis-Stewart. Thank you

Chase Kamp. Thank you Cassandra Gillig. Thank you to my family. Thank you to all my friends and crushes. Thank you to everyone who has included a poem of mine in their magazine or asked me to read in their series. Thank you particularly to Zach Halberg at *Newest York* for publishing an excerpt of "Laura's Desires," and to Rebekah Smith for publishing another excerpt in her zine, *What A Time To Be Alive*, which she scattered across the country on a road trip, as well as to Belladonna* (especially James Loop and Zoe Tuck) for publishing another excerpt as a beautiful golden chaplet. Thank you to Denis Paul and G.E.M. Anscombe for translating *On Certainty* and Emma Crawford and Mario von der Ruhr for translating *Gravity and Grace*. Thank you to New York, California, Arizona, and Tennessee. Thank you to Morgan.

LAURA HENRIKSEN is the author of numerous chapbooks, including *Agata*, *Canadian Girlfriends*, and *October Poems*. Her writing can be found in *Literary Hub*, *The Brooklyn Rail*, and other places. She lives in Sunset Park, Lenapehoking, works at The Poetry Project, and teaches at Pratt. *Laura's Desires* is her first book.

NIGHTBOAT BOOKS

Nightboat Books, a nonprofit organization, seeks to develop audiences for writers whose work resists convention and transcends boundaries. We publish books rich with poignancy, intelligence, and risk. Please visit nightboat.org to learn about our titles and how you can support our future publications.

The following individuals have supported the publication of this book. We thank them for their generosity and commitment to the mission of Nightboat Books:

Kazim Ali • Anonymous (8) • Mary Armantrout • Jean C. Ballantyne • Thomas Ballantyne • Bill Bruns • John Cappetta • V. Shannon Clyne • Ulla Dydo Charitable Fund • Photios Giovanis • Amanda Greenberger • Vandana Khanna • Isaac Klausner • Shari Leinwand • Anne Marie Macari • Elizabeth Madans • Martha Melvoin • Caren Motika • Elizabeth Motika • The Leslie Scalapino - O Books Fund • Robin Shanus • Thomas Shardlow • Rebecca Shea • Ira Silverberg • Benjamin Taylor • David Wall • Jerrie Whitfield & Richard Motika • Arden Wohl • Issam Zineh

This book is made possible, in part, by grants from the New York City Department of Cultural Affairs in partnership with the City Council and the New York State Council on the Arts Literature Program.